BODY
Whispering

A New Way of Seeing, Being & Healing

DR. DAIN HEER

Original Title: *Body Whispering*

Copyright © 2021 Dr. Dain Heer

Access Consciousness Publishing

www.accessconsciousnesspublishing.com

Paperback ISBN#: 978-1-63493-487-9

Ebook ISBN#: 978-1-63493-488-6

Cover Art by: Audrey Denson

Cover Image: Alannah Avelin

Interior Design by: Zoe Norvell

GRATITUDE

You may think you were the one that chose to read this book. I am pretty sure you were not. There is, quite possibly, something way more potent at work here: YOUR BODY. You, my friend, just get to go along for the ride.

For so long, we've been ignoring our bodies' awarenesses and capacities. Now, they are awakening.

Our bodies are hearing the call from the Earth and the world around us, and their whispers are becoming louder every day.

This book is your invitation to become a body whisperer (to find out what that truly means, you'll have to read the book). During this journey, I will do my best to show you what I started to become aware of many years ago when I realized that bodies talked to me. All the time. Very loudly.

It will sound different for you than it does for me, but the basics still apply. The very first step is acknowledging that yes, bodies do talk — just not in words.

I would like to thank my body for showing me what is truly possible, and to simultaneously apologize to it for how long it took me to start to listen.

I would like to thank every single body that I have had the honor and pleasure of meeting, working on, playing with, and learning from, these past 20-plus years. In truth, everybody I've ever met, every hug and every session I've ever gifted or received, has contributed to this book.

Finally, I would like to thank Gary Douglas. Meeting him and doing the very first session of what I now call *The Energetic Synthesis of Being* more than 20 years ago introduced me to the true capacities that we and our bodies have available together.

Without that invitation, my body and I may never have become the co-creators we are today.

Gary often says that everything he has ever learned, he learned from a horse. For me, every step into greatness I've ever taken has started with a whisper from my body.

Is now the time for you to meet your body? For real?

Alas, it begins.

And the Earth (and all the bodies inhabiting it) are rejoicing.

—Dain

Contents

INTRODUCTION

Hands Up If You're A Body Whisperer

At the start of nearly every class or workshop I facilitate, I ask the question above. Some people throw their hands up right away, others raise them tentatively. And a few don't raise their hands at all.

What about you — are you a body whisperer?

Did something inside you just say . . . *Yes?*

It's interesting to consider *when* someone becomes a body whisperer — or a healer, or a facilitator — whichever term you prefer. Is it when you have a practice? Is it when you're being paid? Is it when you have solid, cast-iron proof that you healed, cured, or improved someone's life?

Or do you become a body whisperer when you choose to recognize you've been one all along? What if that is why you are here right now, reading this book?

Let me start by welcoming you appropriately....

Welcome and hello, body whisperer!

Hello to those who can comfortably say it, and hello to those who have an inkling, a spark of an idea that there's a different way of being with their own bodies and the bodies of others.

Hello to those who've been walking this path for years: the practitioners and facilitators working with energy, the massage therapists, reiki practitioners and acupuncturists; the doctors who work in ER, the psychologists, the nurses, the people on the frontline.

Hello to each and every one of you desiring to make a change in your own world and the world of others.

I am so grateful you are here, even if you don't think you fit into any of the categories above.

This book is very dear to my heart. The concepts, stories, tools and techniques shared on these pages are borne of — and connected to — my own personal journey as change-maker: a 20-year joyous ride in which I've facilitated and witnessed phenomenal change in my own body and the bodies of hundreds of thousands of people.

What I'm sharing is a totally different paradigm for healing, change and transformation. The beautiful thing is you can use any and all of the tools in this book alongside the training or techniques you personally favor, and they will only accelerate and expand the change you can create.

Do you realize that initiating change in people's bodies can be easy, effortless, fluid and … fun?

Do you know you can step into a space of being — a space where you get awarenesses and insights that have the capacity to change and create entire worlds? When you see that kind of change in front of your eyes, it feels nothing short of miraculous. You experience a high that's intense, with an undercurrent of peace: because you're doing exactly what you came here to do.

Your space of being is uniquely yours. You have the capacity to offer others a healing change just by them being in your presence.

If, while you're reading (even now, maybe?) the ideas or concepts in this book seem abstract or hard to get or understand — know this: It's okay. You don't need to try so hard to 'get it.' Read on and enjoy the process. Let the pieces fall into place. Pick up what works for you, leave what doesn't. Experiment, play. Be open, and your life and your practice might just become more malleable, dynamic and joyous.

Here's how it worked for me.

Twenty years ago, I was a chiropractor living in one of the most affluent and beautiful places in the world, and I was engaged to be married to a woman who seemed perfect for me. On paper I had it all. In practice, I was a wreck: unhappy and totally unconnected to who I truly was and what I really desired.

Despite being on the cusp of opening my second chiropractic practice, I knew deep down I just wasn't creating the kind of change that had inspired me to become a doctor in the first place. I was unfulfilled and I was desperate — so desperate I set a date to take my own life — unless things changed drastically. And change they did: I discovered the tools of Access Consciousness, and I stepped into my true capacities as *me*. I was able to let go of so much that had been limiting me — including the relationship that seemed so right for me but was far from it. I discovered my true potency as the creator of my own life, and inevitably, gloriously — all of this changed how I worked on people's bodies, too.

Within a very short space of time of using the Access Consciousness tools, I started seeing the miracles I always wanted to create in my chiropractic practice. I developed a modality called Energetic Synthesis of Being (ESB) while working on Gary Douglas, the founder of Access, which I still use and teach others to use today. I became the co-creator of the Access Consciousness movement, and my life has never been the same since — in the best way imaginable. Each day my life continues to change and evolve and expand in incredible ways. So, I don't say this lightly: The tools of Access Consciousness not only changed my life — they *saved* my life.

If you allow them, they could have a world-shifting impact on your life and your practice too.

Do you know you're treading a new path?

It's possible that the tools on these pages are unlike anything you've come across before. As you read, there'll be ideas and concepts that speak to you right away and you'll find yourself nodding eagerly or even saying, "Yes, absolutely!" out loud. Read those things over and over.

There may also be concepts that you'll scrutinize and say, "Yeah, right!" Read *those* things again, too. Why? Because there's a chance that within the concepts you want to distance yourself from, there's a gift for you. Some nugget or awareness of what you can change to make your life and your practice far more dynamic than it's ever been before.

Thank you for being willing to be and explore something different. And when I say different, I mean *totally* different. You're opening the doors to a space very few people have been willing to go. You're at the leading edge of healing, participating in conversations that very few people on this planet are having. Yet!

We'll start our journey with you: by developing a communion with your own body and understanding what a gift it is. Our bodies don't exist in isolation. As you create a greater connection with you and your body, you'll also create a greater connection with other people's bodies. There's no right or wrong way to be a body whisperer: It's something you already are. If anything, we're only undoing where you haven't been able to be it . . . yet.

We'll challenge traditional views of how to heal people, and we'll lift the lid on what creates disease, pain and discomfort. We'll look at the role of presence, chaos and questions in healing. We'll explore the frontiers of working with people, and of consciousness. We'll explore possibilities that others might call off-beat, different or even weird. And that's fine with me. When you experience the change for yourself, you might find you're fine with weird, too.

No one is greater than you. There's no reason why you can't discover things on these pages and beyond that I'm not aware of yet. It's a glorious joint effort — so thank you for joining me. I am so excited to see the change *you* will create.

Shall we begin?

PART
ONE

A NEW
WAY TO
SEE

What if you could have an instant connection to every molecule in the universe?

—

What if you have an inner guidance system which, once you tap into it, can lead you toward the greatest choices for your life and living?

—

Is it time to explore the concept of consciousness, and live from a place of gifting, receiving and no judgment?

—

These first two chapters form the foundation for everything else; all that is required of you is to read with open eyes and an open mind.

ENERGY

Relearning Your First Language

Let's begin by taking a moment to think about the many and varied ways we communicate with each other on this beautiful planet we currently inhabit.

What kind of methods of communication come to mind? How do we tell each other who we are, what we need, where we're going, or where we've been?

We use our voices to speak — in person, over the phone, sometimes via video calling.

We write — on paper and electronically. We send instant messages, share statuses online, write emails. We pen letters if we're feeling traditional, or we write books if we have something big to share. I love the fact I wrote this book several months ago, maybe even years ago if you're coming to it a little later — and here you are: hearing me across time. You could be reading these words on a paper page or on a screen; you could even be listening to the audio book.

Some of us draw, paint or make music to tell others who we are and what's important to us.

When we're face-to-face we don't just use speech, we use body language too: We widen our eyes in shock, or we roll them in frustration. We fold our arms when we're wary, or we throw them in the air when we're excited.

You could say we've got verbal, written and physical communication down to a fine art!

What if there's another way to speak, converse, communicate?

What if we have so much more available to us than we realize?

And what if accessing it could change our lives in phenomenal ways?

Energy is your body's first language, and it's *your* first language

Have you ever walked into a room and knew, in a second, that whoever was in that room was annoyed with you? Maybe it was your partner, your mom, your sister, your boss. Even before they said a word or made eye contact with you, even in the second you touched the door handle to enter the room — you knew they were harboring a resentment or a judgment.

How? Because you sensed it, felt it, *knew* it — and it was their energy that communicated it to you.

Here's another way energy speaks to us. Do you have someone in your life who's really in tune with you, really gets you, and just from saying "Hi," over the phone they'll know you have something difficult going on in your life? Your words might say you're fine, but your friend is hearing something else; they're hearing your energy.

It's quick, instant, natural ... and you can have that instantaneous connection, that common language, with *everything* in the universe. Everything.

Including, *or especially* — your body. It's just a case of choosing to tune in and practicing this skill you've been unaware of until now.

It starts with you.

Heavy or light

If you're new to thinking about energy in this way, the first step is to start noticing your own energy. Once you begin to become aware of it, you'll wonder how you ever missed it.

Let me ask you this: Roughly speaking, when something feels good to you, when you're excited, or relieved, or happy, or at peace: Do you feel *heavy or light?*

Light, right?

When you're worried about something, or scared, or sad, or anxious: Do you feel *heavy or light?*

My guess is heavy.

Another way of looking at it might be, when you're happy, do you sense your energy is expanding? And when you're sad, do you sense your energy is contracted, or maybe compressed?

What I'm working toward is the idea that you know when something is right for you, or, a better way of putting it is *true for you*, when you feel a sense of expansion —

a lightness — around it. When something is not right for you, or a lie for you, you feel constricted — or heavy.

The sensation of heavy and light is different for everyone, so I can't tell you exactly what it feels like, but you can get to know what it is for you.

Some people describe light feeling like a joyful burst, or a steady smile, or a feeling of growth and possibility. Heavy might feel like you're tired, or a dead weight, or confined.

See heavy or light as your inner guidance system. Get to know your guidance system first by noticing it. When you're around someone you don't click with, notice it. When you're around someone you feel relaxed with, notice it. When you're about to do something that you love doing, notice it.

When you're about to do something that scares you, notice it — and this might surprise you. You can often feel light even when you're about to do something terrifying. Why? Because energetically, excitement and fear feel pretty much the same. If you are light, you can be pretty sure that what you think is fear, is actually excitement. The energy has spoken!

My advice is not to overthink it, just start to tap into the incredible inner awareness that you naturally have.

DO YOU KNOW...?

Every molecule in the universe has consciousness: every plant, every raindrop, every gust of wind. Every animal, every tree, every gemstone, every rock. Every building, every car, every piece of machinery. Every person, every thing.

Every *body*.

My body, your body, the bodies you work with, the bodies you know: They all have consciousness.

This isn't a new discovery; Einstein acknowledged the consciousness of every molecule and every element in the universe. And — here's the key part — he recognized that these conscious molecules communicate with each other, *all the time*.

And how? With your first language. The language that is more sophisticated and more instantaneous than words: energy.

Is it possible that your body has been trying to communicate with you for a long, long time?

And what would happen if you were to start listening?

CONSCIOUSNESS

The Key To Creating Change

Consciousness is a concept that can appear hard to understand and yet simultaneously easy to know.

It only gets tricky when we try to wrap our heads around it! The mind gets too involved and grasps for meaning and sense. The thing about the human mind is that it has this excessive need to relate new concepts to other concepts that it already gets and is familiar with, then it can add the new concept to the box labeled, "Things I Understand Perfectly."

The way I describe consciousness may be very different from what you are used to. Simply read with an open mind, and as you read, listen to your inner guidance:

Notice if what I'm talking about opens up new possibilities for you, and if you get a sense of heavy or light.

In consciousness, everything exists, and nothing is judged

Being conscious is a choice, rather than a status that you achieve, or a level you attain. It's already in you, around you, and available to you. It may just be that until now you weren't able to choose it, because you didn't realize it was a possibility.

It's about oneness. It's about the allowance of everything, everyone, every choice, and never judging any of those things.

In consciousness, there's no separation. You are receiving everything, the good, the bad, the ugly. Only you don't need to categorize them in such a way; in consciousness, the polarities of good and bad are no longer the driving force for your life and living.

The perfect trap

One of the myths of this reality is that judgment is necessary to create a functioning world. We've been taught that we must judge to get this reality right: Judgment is how we approach everything from relationships to work, culture, spirituality, health and bodies. Most of us spend our whole lives convinced that we're wrong while trying desperately to be or convince ourselves that we are right.

It becomes a perfect trap.

What if none of that is true or real? What if judgment is one of the biggest limitations there is? What if any time you decide something is good, bad, right, or wrong, you limit you, you limit the thing or person that you're judging, you limit what you can receive, and you make your world (and the world) smaller?

Some argue that the path to freedom is to see everyone and everything as good. I understand that idea; I was a subscriber to it for a long time. It comes from a place of trying to create a kinder, gentler, greater world. But it creates a big problem: To see everything as good, we have to cut off our awareness of everything that doesn't fit into that mold. And that's a lot of stuff!

Consciousness, on the other hand, includes everything and everyone; it judges nothing and no one. If you're truly going to be conscious, you have to be willing to see the good, the bad and the ugly that someone — or you — are currently choosing, as well as the capacity everyone has to choose something different. And see all of that with no point of view or agenda.

If our parents and teachers really wanted to teach us how to navigate the world more easily, they could have asked us, *"What are you aware of here? What will this create if you choose it?"*

That way, we could have learned to use our awareness to create what we would like — rather than using our judgment to conclude what to avoid.

The clearing statement: Accelerator of change

Are you ready to be introduced to one of the weirdest, wackiest and most dynamic tools of Access Consciousness?

We call it **The Clearing Statement**, which is actually a very literal and straight-forward name for it — because it has the capacity to clear whatever is blocking you, limiting you, and keeping you from your true greatness and your natural state.

What is your natural state? It's one of possibilities, potency, happiness and ease, and the clearing statement gets you to those places faster than anything else I know.

Here it is:

> *Right and wrong, good and bad, POD & POC, all 9,*
> *shorts, boys and beyonds.*

If it's your first time seeing those words, it's very likely your mind has gone, "Er, what?" and that's okay! You don't actually need to cognitively know or understand what these words mean (radical, right?) for them to create change in your energy and your life.

But I know how the mind likes answers, and if you would like a breakdown of those words and phrases, they are available to you toward the back of the book — you can head there now if you like.

Did you go? Did you come back? Awesome.

The quickest way to get an understanding of the clearing statement is to see how it works in action, which we'll be doing in just a second. Before we do, a good thing to know is that the clearing statement always follows a question — because questions bring up energy *and* they have a brilliant capacity to open our worlds to the possibility of change.

So, here's a question for you:

What have you bought as true about you that actually isn't true, and that is keeping you small?

Notice what energy that brings up: That's always the first step. Get the energy of the question without looking for any definite answers or conclusions.

The next part of the process involves asking another question — usually, it's along the lines of: *Would you be willing to destroy and uncreate all of that?* In other words — are you willing to give up what's limiting you — all the feelings, thoughts, emotions, judgments, conclusions and computations, and everything else that you put in place that keep you from being as big, bold and beautiful as you truly are?

In essence what we're doing is paving the way for the clearing statement:

> *Right and wrong, good and bad, POD & POC, all 9, shorts, boys and beyonds.*

because the clearing statement is what destroys and uncreates whatever came up when we asked that first question.

Notice the words in the question right before the clearing statement: *Will you now* — this is the key part. For the clearing statement to do its thing, you have to be willing to *allow it* to do its thing. YOU have to choose in order for something to change. Sometimes you will be absolutely willing and ready, and you'll obliterate all the walls, barriers, restrictions and limitations that came up, and other times you might need to run the question and the clearing statement a few or a few dozen times to start to feel the space and freedom it brings.

A small note: Don't try to know it or "get it" or feel really definite about this. When you ask if you're willing to destroy and uncreate, you're asking YOU, and it's your choice — and one that goes way beyond your cognitive mind. It's a choice made by your being.

Here's the full version of the example we just looked at. You might want to run it in its entirety and notice what happens with the energy you tap into.

> _What have you bought as true about you that actually isn't, and that is keeping you small?_
>
> _Will you destroy and uncreate all of that?_ **_Right and wrong, good and bad, POD & POC, all 9, shorts, boys and beyonds._**

My advice is to play with using the clearing statement when it comes up in the course of this book. Because what if it works? What if it easily, swiftly and effortlessly creates changes and shifts in your world, your body — your being — that you never imagined were possible?

You may be wondering....

Do I have to use the clearing statement in order to create change?

Not necessarily. See it as an accelerator, a tool that can open your world and expand your horizons. Without it, you can still understand that some of your points of view may have been holding you back, but with it you can change them — and you can change them in a beat.

Do I have to say the words out loud?

The clearing statement works whether you say it out loud, or quietly under your breath, or silently in your head. It also works if you use the abridged version: "POD and POC it," which stands for point of destruction, point of creation.

Sorry what? Point of creation, point of destruction?

That's us asking the energy to go back to wherever it came from so we can be free of its limitations and choose something else. POD and POC are the superheroes of consciousness. They undo wherever you created something that limited you (POC), or where you destroyed something that could create more for you (POD). There may not be one single place of origin for the energy that you're clearing — there may be a billion, a trillion of them, or even a godzillion of them.

A godzillion?

A godzillion is a number so big only God knows. It's sort of like steroids for the clearing statement. You'll notice it sometimes appears in the clearing statement — it really ramps its potency up!

As a practicing healer, can I use the clearing statement when I work on other people?

Absolutely, I'll give you some ways to use it as we venture through the book. If you choose to say it out loud, and you want to let people know it came from this book or Access Consciousness, that's great — and also you don't have to.

In essence, the clearing statement is based on the idea that everything is changeable. Look at something solid in the room you're in; the wall, a table, a coffee cup, a vase. They look pretty solid, don't they? Yet science tells us everything is actually 99.99% space. Those things appear solid, because the molecules have arranged themselves that way, and our point of view, and our expectations, keep them arranged that way too.

What if everything in your life were changeable? Including, and especially — your limitations — which seem so solid and real?

What if you could access the space that is within that solidity and walk right through those limitations?

Using the clearing statement beyond the pages of this book

Sometimes, as you're experiencing life, you'll perceive a limiting energy around a situation, a person, or an event. You could be on your way to a business meeting, feeling apprehensive or anxious about how your ideas will be received. That energy — the heavy, restrictive energy — can be cleared with a POD & POC.

Or, you could be about to do something you've been looking forward to for days or months — maybe you're on your way to dinner with your best friend, or you're about to go on retreat to your favorite place in the world, where you've been a dozen times already — and you get that restrictive, solid energy and you have no idea why. You don't need to know why it's there to clear it, and you don't need to know where it came from. Notice the energy and use the abridged version: "POD & POC it, POD & POC it, POD & POC it."

The brilliance of the clearing statement — and the reason I often call it 'The Magic Wand,' is that it works to change anything that's limiting you, and you don't need to spend hours in therapy, and you never have to analyze or scrutinize yourself. The limiting belief that you're undoing might be something you created last week, last year, or in a previous lifetime. Doesn't matter. You can change it now.

That's the power the clearing statement has: It allows you to use the malleable chaos of consciousness to create a new reality.

PART
TWO

A NEW
WAY
TO BE

Your journey as a body whisperer has begun, with the introduction of energy and consciousness.

—

What if reawakening the connection with your own body is the catalyst for everything that follows?

—

What if you were willing to know how the body uses pain and discomfort to communicate with us?

—

What if you could lift the veil on the root cause of all disease, and with that awareness, you could bring a healing change to your own body, and those you work with?

—

What would be possible then?

Listening And Talking To Your Body

Take a moment to think about how your relationship with your body began, way back in your early childhood. Specifically, recall how mealtimes were for you growing up.

Who decided *when* you ate? Who decided *what* you ate? Who decided *how much* you ate?

Did your parents let you bypass your vegetables and head straight for dessert?

What happened if you were full, but you hadn't eaten everything? What happened if you were hungry outside mealtimes? Was food used as reward for being good or a pacifier when you were being too much? Was clearing your plate taken as a mark of respect to your parents — while also being a sign of compassion to children around the world less fortunate than you?

If you're nodding along to any of this, please know that you were not alone!

Why we stopped listening to our bodies

Restrictions and rules around food are commonplace in most families. Usually it's all very well-meaning, but it's rare that someone stops to think about the message it sends to kids, which is pretty much this: *Listen to how other people think you should nourish your body, rather than trust that your body knows intuitively what nourishment it requires.*

Interestingly, without demands and expectations placed on them, children behave very differently around food. You'll see that they graze: They'll eat a little and then they'll go and play, then they'll come back, then they'll eat some more, and then they'll go and play ... and so on.

The only thing that limits kids from this natural ebb and flow is the adults' rigid point of view that they have to do mealtimes and eating in a certain way.

What if eating more than you need, or eating what your body has no interest in consuming, are just two of the ways you may have been practiced out of listening to what your body is trying to tell you?

What if there are a dozen more? Or maybe more like a thousand more?

Who are you choosing for?

Consider this: When you get dressed in the morning, and you're there in front of your closet, selecting your outfit for the day, *who are you choosing for?*

Are you choosing for you? Or are you choosing with others in mind?

Do you factor in what other people will think of what you're wearing when you make your choice — perhaps the people at work, or your partner, or your Mom ... and then do you get all caught up in what you think you *should* wear, and disregard what you would *like* to wear?

More specifically — do you disregard what *your body* would like to wear?

Because yes — your body absolutely has a point of view about the clothes you put on it!

We just never thought of asking.

Why is that? Well, in exactly the same way that we grew up receiving messages about what food we should consume, we were also inundated with opinions and points of view about what clothes were acceptable and appropriate for us to wear.

Think about it, did you ever get a disapproving look from your parents for an outfit you chose as a teenager? And what about now?

If you're like a lot of the people I know and work with, chances are you still get those side-eyes or thinly veiled criticisms at family get-togethers about your appearance:

Oh, that's an interesting look, honey.

Is that dress actually your size?

How would you describe that color?

Other people's unsolicited opinions are fired at us, directly or indirectly, every moment of the day. Think about the media: Those magazines and online articles are awash with advice about what to wear and what not to wear. What's hot this season, what's not. After any high-profile award ceremony, you'll find a dissection of the outfits worn on the red carpet — some will be celebrated, others mocked.

Why am I talking about all of this?

Well — think about all of those judgments and points of view — just about the garments we put on our bodies!

We soak it all up and never once stop to ask what our bodies require.

Your body's awareness doesn't end at matters relating to food and clothes: It also has awarenesses about the activities it likes to participate in, who it likes to be around, and who it desires to get intimate with.

Whenever we keep the volume turned up on the judgments, points of view and conclusions of others, and turn the volume down on our own bodies, we keep ourselves separate from its incredible and gentle awarenesses ... *about everything.*

What does your body have to do to get your attention?

What happens when we DON'T listen to our bodies?

When you're separate from your body, and out of practice with the energetic language it uses, it simply has to find another way to tell you what it needs to tell you. This is why the body creates stiffness, pain and disease — all as a way of getting our attention, all as a way to communicate whatever awareness we're not listening to.

Now, we're going to explore this a lot more as we go through the book, but just take a second to think about this.

There's almost a sadness to it: Our bodies are so giving. Just think about what they do for us each and every day: They take us from A to B to Z, they digest food, fight bugs, circulate blood and oxygen … they're pretty much running the whole physical show! And here we are, so oblivious that it's got to the stage where pain and stiffness are the only ways they can reach out to us.

The amazing and world-shifting news is that you can develop a relationship with your body today, starting right now if you choose. This relationship can be nurtured and built upon with ease, and the whole process will contribute to your life, your living AND your business and practice.

Ready to unlock some doors right now?

Shall we use the clearing statement? It really is the quickest way I've ever found to change anything and everything. This one is focused on destroying and uncreating all those right and wrong points of view about what your body needs or desires.

Here it is. Read it and notice the energy it conjures.

> *Everything you've done to impose there's a right or wrong point of view about eating, about supplementation, about clothes, about all the other things that your body desires or doesn't, whether it's an amount of*

sleep you've decided your body needs to have, whether it's a particular food it needs to eat, will you destroy and uncreate it now please? **Right and wrong, good and bad, POD & POC, all 9, shorts, boys and beyonds.**

How was that? You might want to run it a couple of times, and just notice what happens to the energy that comes up. Notice how it expands, as if more space appears around it. That's you clearing your limiting points of view. Go you!

We can talk for hours and we will move forward, or we can use the clearing statement and move mountains.

Unconsciousness and Anti-Consciousness: The Basis of all Disease

All disease, whether it's physical or psychological, whether it presents itself as pain, illness, tiredness or malaise, is a result of one or both of these two states: unconsciousness and anti-consciousness — and judgment is the crucial ingredient in both of those states. We're going to talk more about the effects of judgment throughout the book — particularly in Chapter 5. I often refer to judgment as a killer: It's a killer of possibility, and of change.

If we go back to the notion that consciousness is where everything exists and nothing is judged, and where nothing is made right and nothing is made wrong, then we can get a little closer to understanding unconsciousness and anti-consciousness. Let's continue to unpick and unpack what they are, and how they relate to disease.

Unconsciousness is akin to unawareness. It's how we live when we haven't realized our capacity for greatness, and when we haven't recognized our capacity to see through the lies of the reality we've been sold. We're not ready, or willing, to see the full spectrum of possibilities that are available to us. We live in a narrow way, governed, and blinded, by judgment.

Anti-consciousness is similar in the way that judgment is what fuels it, and it's similar in the way that the person doing anti-consciousness is closed off to how incredible their life could be, but unlike unconsciousness, there's an element of choice involved.

It's akin to self-sabotage: Someone who's anti-conscious, for whatever reason, has made the decision to undo or step away from consciousness, even though they know, on some level, that doing so will limit them personally.

It's important to note that anti-consciousness can also be directed at others. Again, it often gets fired in the form of judgments, and when you realize this, you'll get wise to other people's judgments invading your world and your being. Gratefully we can be armed and ready!

Or, more accurately: We can be *aware* of anti-consciousness — and that's where our power lies.

When we're aware, and conscious ourselves, we become impermeable to other people's judgments and general anti-consciousness. And, here's the great part: Our bodies become a lot lighter, and a lot healthier. And way happier.

Pain, stiffness, disease — it's all a result of unconsciousness and anti-consciousness. When you start to get that, you can start using this awareness to create more space in your body and in the bodies of others.

Ready for the science bit?

Ellipticals

Your cells, when they are healthy, are spherical in structure. As spheres, they are open and absorbent. As spheres, they do what they need to do to keep us highly functioning and free from disease, and they do it well.

In recent years, scientists have discovered that the spherical structure of a cell is jeopardized, *and changed*, by thoughts, feelings and emotions. Our judgments and points of view can actually alter the energetic matrix of a cell from spherical to elliptical, and, here's the key: An elliptical cell structure is, scientists say, the basis for disease. This includes stiffness, pain and any other physical presentations — and any psychological presentations too.

Do you get the magnitude of that? The judgments we harbor, whether they are ours or given to us (we'll go into that more deeply later in the book) actually get locked into our cells, into our bodies and manifest as disease.

Judgment locks our bodies up.

The good news is — we have the keys to unlock our bodies, and much more.

Our remedy is always, always, always consciousness. With consciousness you bring yourself, and the people you work on, to the awareness of something, and in taking away the element of judgment you free them — literally free them

— from whatever has been holding them back. Shoulder pain, back pain, tiredness, lethargy, depression ... the list is endless.

In consciousness, dynamic changes occur.

When you choose consciousness for you, you not only change your own life, but you also get to offer it as an option to the people you work with and on.

And when you couple consciousness with the clearing statement, your capacity to empower people to dissolve any unconsciousness and anti-consciousness that they've locked into their cells, their body and their life, is limitless.

What happens when we DO listen to our bodies?

When you start listening and talking to bodies — your own and others — you move away from predicting, assuming and judging what they require. You start listening with openness and without any fixed points of view or judgments.

Your awareness accelerates. There's an easy alertness to how you are with people. You gain insights in a flash that talking, and thinking, may never have led you to.

As your relationship with your body develops, you'll undo so much that has been causing you pain and keeping you static.

If you're a practicing healer, your clients will love coming to you because you'll contribute in phenomenal ways to their life and living. And when you're that effective, word can't help but spread — your clients will tell anyone who'll listen how awesome you are (and how they can schedule an appointment with you).

In short, you become a beacon to the people around you — not just your clients, but also your family, your friends and anyone you interact with. At Access we realized a long time ago that consciousness is contagious. Let's use this to our advantage and create an epidemic of awareness!

Are you ready to reawaken your natural connection to every molecule around you? To listen with more and more ease, and to unlock doors that have been closed and cemented up for years?

Get this: You're already on the path. Just by reading this book, and being open to the ideas within it, you're on your way.

Ready to go further?

You and your body: Developing a communion

For me, the word communion speaks of a sense of connection, which is why I've chosen it here. We're honing and developing that natural and beautiful communion between you: the being, and your physical self: your body.

Developing a communion with your body begins with asking your body questions and doing so from an open and present place. And then ... listening.

Sound easy? Sound hard?

Wait, in some way — could you know all this already?

Is this old news, or new news which somehow feels familiar, like pieces of a puzzle falling into place...?

Could it be possible that you've always known that your body has consciousness, and today is the day you can become truly aware of it?

Our starting point is asking our body about everything that concerns it: from the food it eats, to the clothes it wears, to the people it gets intimate with.

Are you thinking, *So where am I in all of this?*

You, alert and conscious reader, are an infinite being. You just happen to take form in this particular body, or vehicle, you occupy right now. If I can be blunt about it: Long after your body expires, after it's in the ground, or turned to ashes, YOU, the being, will continue.

Recognizing that you're an infinite being is crucial to developing the communion you can have with your body, but acknowledging this is sometimes not easy…. Let's explore it a little more.

Three steps to developing a communion with your body

Step 1: Understanding that you are infinite

I'd like to share an exercise with you which is wonderful for getting the sense of this concept of you being an infinite being. I recommend you read it through a couple of times then take a moment to try it yourself.

Begin by expanding 100 miles out in all directions. Close your eyes if you like and expand outwards. It's not your physical body that's expanding — it's your energy, your being.

Expand your being out in all directions, 100 miles.

Notice that you can do that easily, quickly.

When you're there, go a further 100 miles in all directions.

Notice that you can. Notice how you can be where you choose to be.

Next go 1,000 miles past that, in all directions. Notice you're there too.

Now go 100,000 miles in all directions.

See how infinite you are?

—

How was that?

Oftentimes, that exercise results in a beautiful, big, deep breath as you — at last — occupy the space you'd like to occupy as a being!

For some of you, this might be the first time you've realized you have that capacity, for others it might have been the thousandth time.

If you're anything like me, it never gets any less awesome.

I have to ask: If a being can go out and be that expansive, travel so far in an instant, be that big — could it ever fit inside of a physical body the size of yours?

I think not.

The notion that we start and end in our physical bodies is one of the most limiting beliefs we're sold, and the worst part is that in thinking we are only as big, or small, as our bodies, we resent having one — because we know, somewhere in us, that we're huge — yet we keep pretending that we're not.

Now that you've sampled with such ease your capacity as an infinite being, are you ready to really let go of the big one: the limiting belief that you are limited by your body?

> *All the points of view that you bought that you're actually limited by your body, rather than you can have the amazingly large space that you as an infinite being are, and still have your body, will you destroy and uncreate it please?* ***Right and wrong, good and bad, POD & POC, all 9, shorts, boys and beyonds.***

> *Everything you've done to pretend that you're only this big, which is an invalidation of your being, which also causes you to resent your body and be angry with your body, as though it's your body's fault that you chose to pretend you're only this big, will you destroy and uncreate it please?* ***Right and wrong, good and bad, POD & POC, all 9, shorts, boys and beyonds.***

Run those clearings and take a beautiful deep breath.

You are infinite, and as big as you want to be. You have instant access to an astonishing sense of space — the kind of openness that allows you to breathe easily and freely. You can ask to *be* that space in any moment of any day.

What does this mean for your body?

When you play with the idea that your body is your vehicle for this lifetime, you still get to have a connection to it, but the space of your being is no longer limited by it.

You can lose any underlying resentments you had toward your body when you felt captive in it, and from the space of your being you can contribute to your body in phenomenal ways.

How? Well, what if you could reach out right now across the planet? You did it a couple of pages ago. You can do it whenever you choose. It might seem like a bizarre concept at first, but if you could reach all the way across the planet and tap into every mountain, every tree, every stream, every river, every ocean, every bird … what would that be like?

How much peace would it bring your body?

How much vitality, strength and healing would that bring to your body?

And what if you were to access all of that, while you were working on people's bodies? What would be possible then?

Step 2: Start asking, start listening

Once you accept that you're an infinite being in a temporary physical body — a body which is conscious, and aware, and would like to be in harmony with you, you get closer to the idea that:

Your body eats, you as a being don't eat.

Your body wears clothes, you as a being don't wear clothes.

Your body has sex, you as a being don't. (Well, hopefully you're there too!)

This might feel a lot to take in — don't worry! Don't judge yourself if it's not feeling light or right for you just yet. If you can begin to contemplate the idea that your body has its own points of view which so far you may not have asked for, for now that is awesome.

If you'd like more clarity with it, run this:

> _Everything that doesn't allow you to begin to ask your_
> _body for everything that concerns it, will you destroy_
> _and uncreate it please?_ **Right and wrong, good and**
> **bad, POD & POC, all 9, shorts, boys and beyonds.**

When it comes to asking your body what it requires, I recommend you start with something really simple, such as food.

Remember, your body eats, you don't, so it makes sense to inquire!

Let's say you're at breakfast. You're in your house and you walk into the kitchen, and instead of automatically reaching for your usual breakfast item, what if instead you took a moment to ask, _Body, what would you like to eat?_

Then: Be open, be present and listen.

Ask again: _Body, what would you like to eat?_

What do you sense? What are you picking up? Your body might want eggs, or bacon, or cheese, or fruit ... or all of the above, or none of the above.

Your body might not be hungry yet. You don't have to autopilot-eat just because it's a conventional or accepted mealtime. And you don't have to restrict yourself to traditional breakfast items either. What if your body would like that leftover pasta? Or ice cream? Or pasta and then ice cream?

Would it be okay to give that to your body at 8 am?

There's only one way to find out ... and there are no rights and no wrongs here — only interesting choices. And cold pasta and ice cream is definitely an interesting breakfast choice!

Don't expect yourself to get it right or perfect immediately. Imagine you wanted to go from having never run a day in your life to participating in a marathon — would you just get up and run 27 miles or would you practice first? It's the same here. Only it's a lot easier!

It's through practice that you'll start to pick up the energetic insistence your body has.

Next, try it with clothes. When you're starting the day, stand in front of your closet, and say, *Body, what would you like to wear today?*

Again, be present, be open and listen.

You might find that what your body wants to wear is the last thing you would have chosen to wear if you hadn't asked! You might find yourself reaching into some dark corner of your closet for something you haven't worn in years, and when you put it on and look in the mirror — it lights you up. It lights your body up. Why? Because that's the thing your body wants to wear!

When you wear what your body wants to wear, you keep that light on all day. You feel alive all day. People will give you more compliments than you've ever gotten before.

Why is there a difference between what you, the being, might choose to wear, and what your body might choose to wear?

Simply: What you think and choose is based on your judgments, your projections, your expectations and your points of view about what's right and what's wrong. Your body brings none of that to the table.

Your body could have totally different points of view and insights — and you'll never know unless you ask.

Now, if you're not perfect doing this the first time, or the second time, or the tenth time, or the hundredth time, please don't make yourself wrong. You're developing a completely new relationship, a completely new connection with your body that you haven't had before. Well — you did have it, but like the rest of us, you weren't taught to nurture it, so it was out of reach for a while.

As well as asking your body what it would like to eat and wear, you can also ask:

Who would you like to have sex with?

What would you like to do today?

What kind of movement would you like to do?

Is it time to start having fun breathing new life into this connection?

Step 3: Be patient

Have you ever had a really good friend, one who you felt a deep and joyful connection with? One of those friendships where you can totally be who you are, no masks, no playing a part that doesn't suit you — you just get to be you.

If you were to lose touch with that friend, imagine reconnecting. Imagine calling them up and the years and the distance just melting away and feeling connected again to someone who was such a contribution to you. It might happen instantly, or it might take a little warming up — and it's the same with your body.

The time and effort to start to rebuild the connection is so, so minimal compared to the phenomenal results and rewards you'll receive. And, when you take these tools into the way you practice, you can expect to create unimaginable change.

If you pass the three steps we just explored on to your clients, they'll start to create a connection with their bodies and a oneness where there's just no room for judgment. You can guide them as they bring their body back into the fold of their life and their living, allowing you to facilitate incredible healing and change for them.

My beautiful friends, the adventure has truly begun

Are you ready to commit to building a communion with your body?

For the next three days, would you be willing to ask your body for its point of view about everything that concerns it? Can you acknowledge that your body knows what it requires and what it desires?

The beautiful thing here is that your relationship with your body is a natural part of you and you're simply reawakening it. It's as natural as breathing.

Soon enough you'll be listening and talking to your body without thinking about it and wondering how the two of you ever lost touch.

The Body As A Psychic Receiver

Your body is extremely intuitive. It picks up on the energies of others: their emotions, their judgments, their grievances, their thoughts, their ideas and their pain.

Your body does this to the extent that — get ready for this:

Somewhere between 50 and 100% of what goes on in your physical body (aches, pains, illness) may not even be yours,

And:

98% of what goes on in your mind (your thoughts, feelings, emotions and judgments) don't belong to you.

When I first heard these two figures, it took me a moment

to take them in. Then, when the awareness settled some-what, I experienced a total paradigm shift coupled with a beautiful sense of lightness.

Really? I thought — *almost all of the pain I've experienced isn't even mine?!* I felt a huge sense of liberation.

Is this true for you too? Could a lot of what's in your body and your mind not even be yours? If it is, then like me, and probably every other person reading this book — your beautiful body is beautifully sponge-like!

Knowing this, and being able to work with it, places you at the leading edge of what you do as a healer — *and* it makes living your own life

so

much

easier.

Our bodies are giving us information all the time. Our bodies are sensate, sensorial, sensory mechanisms. You know how a cat's whiskers tell the cat about the world around it? That's what our bodies do for us.

You could pass someone on the street who's having a knee

problem and all of a sudden your own knee will start to hurt. To you it's unexpected, but it's just your body saying, *Hey — that person has a knee problem.* Your body picked up on that person's pain and is telling you about it, and understandably — before you got this awareness — you thought that pain was your own.

I feel it, therefore it's mine

We've been led to believe that everything we're aware of and everything we perceive, in both our bodies and our minds, is ours. There's a sense of, *If I feel it, it must be mine.*

What if it's not?

What if what I'm saying is true, and between 50 and 100% of what goes on in your body came from somewhere or someone else?

What if 98% of your thoughts, feelings, emotions and judgments don't belong to you?

Get the sense of that just for a moment: If you could clear 98% of the thoughts that run around your mind every day, you'd only have to deal with the 2% that are actually yours.

What an amazing gift that would be, what clarity you'd have. And how would that affect and change your day-to-day life and living?

When I came to Access 20 years ago, those two nuggets of awareness were the beginning of a new way of being with my own body, and with the people I worked on, and they have created unimaginable change.

How can you know?

Recognizing that it's a possibility that what you're perceiving in your body and mind might not be yours is one thing, but how can you *know* for sure? How can you know if what you're feeling, like knee pain, or sadness, or anger, or nausea are yours or not?

And if they are yours — what then?

And if they're not yours — what then?

My friend, it's so easy.

First, you can find out if what's troubling you is yours or not by ... asking. Who knew it could be so simple?!

The question that takes you to that awareness is one you want to have in your toolbox, from this moment on, and possibly forever.

Here it is: Who does this belong to?

You can ask, *Who does this belong to?* to anything that you perceive in your body or your mind: any pain, any thought, feeling, judgment, sensation ... literally anything and everything.

With a little practice you'll start to sift and decipher and *know* what's really yours and what's not. And when you know, you can either let it go, or access the awareness you require to let it go.

Let me give you an example. Let's go with the scenario I used a few pages ago — the knee pain picked up from someone in the street. When you first perceive the pain, you don't yet know if it's yours or not, so you ask: *Body, who does this knee pain belong to?*

If you get a sense of lightness, an easing of the pain, a spacious sensation — it's not yours. When it's light, you know your body has picked up the pain and your only requirement here is to return it to sender.

You can do this by saying, *Wow, body thank you so much for the awareness, you sweet creature. Can we let it go now?*

Then follow that with the clearing statement: **Right and wrong, good and bad, POD & POC, all 9, shorts, boys and beyonds.**

It's not your responsibility to identify who the knee pain belongs to or to change it in any way, your only task is to POD & POC it and let it go. As a reminder, when I say, "POD & POC it," I mean use the clearing statement. You can choose to say it in full (as in the example above) or you can use the shorthand, abridged version of "POD & POC it." It works just the same.

The other possibility is your knee hurts, and you get a heavy feeling when you ask, *Who does this knee pain belong to?* If that happens, then you know you either created the pain, or you believed it belonged to you and took it on as yours (maybe as a means of healing it) at some point in the past. Either way, you now have the tools to undo it.

If you created it, it came from a judgment or a fixed point of view. We're going to unpick the whole area of judgment in more depth in the next chapter, and later in the book (Chapter 10) I'll be offering you some practical tools and awarenesses for dealing with pain we created ourselves or are having trouble letting go of, but for now it's enough to know that any pain or discomfort you experience is your body's way of giving you an awareness – and if you created it (rather than picked it up from someone else) then its root is in judgment, or any fixed point of view you have made real for you that isn't.

So, knowing that it's yours, you're now in a great position to access whatever awareness your body is trying to communicate with you, and again, the way to that place is through a question.

You can ask, *What am I not acknowledging that I'm locking into my body as this pain?*

Ask the question and see what comes up for you, but you don't have to get a specific answer in order to clear it. You can just get the energy of it and say, *<u>Everything that won't allow that and allow me to acknowledge it, I now destroy and uncreate it. Times a godzillion.</u>* ***<u>Right and wrong, good and bad, POD & POC, all 9, shorts, boys and beyonds.</u>***

Are you getting what a valuable tool *Who Does This Belong To?* is? It's seriously win-win.

Not yours? You know what to do with it.

Yours? You know what to do with it.

Ready to try it?

Would you be willing to ask, *Who does this belong to?* to any physical pain you perceive, as well as any thoughts, feelings and judgments that you have for the rest of today?

Would you be willing to do it for the next three days?

When this tool was first introduced to me, that's what I did — I used it constantly for three days and I had such a life-changing experience that I wholly recommend you try it for three days too. Seriously, you'll lighten up to such an extent that you'll be like a walking, talking meditation.

In tuning in to what's yours and what isn't, you let go of what you don't need and it feels like you've shed 100 pounds.

Remember, your goal isn't to get a definite answer to the question *Who does this belong to?* It might come to you as an awareness right away, or it might not. It might become obvious before you even finish asking the question:

"Who does this belo— oh, wait a minute ... of course! This is my sister's hang up, not mine."

Or it might stay unknown to you, and that's okay; your only job is to ask the question and perceive the lightness or the heaviness that follows. Once again — if it's light, return it to sender followed with a POD & POC; if it's heavy, ask what you're not acknowledging.

If you do this to every thought, feeling, emotion, judgment and point of view you have for three days, you'll clear everyone else's ideas, points of view and judgments out of your mind, and ... can you sense the blissful freedom just as you contemplate that as a possibility? From there you'll get to function from such a beautifully peaceful and alert place.

I credit *Who Does This Belong To?* with being one of the questions that saved my life. I used it to help cure myself of depression and it's never lost its potency or relevance. It's still a huge part of how I practice and function today. In fact, I use this one tool in almost all of the sessions that I do, and I still use it with myself.

I'd love for you to explore this. Take some time to use *Who Does This Belong To?* on your own body and you'll be setting the course in motion for using it with your clients to unbelievable effect.

We'll be taking a closer look at how in Chapter 10, but for now have fun tuning into and appreciating the beautiful gift of your sensorial physical body.

CHAPTER
5

Letting Go Of Judgment

Here's a question: How many of the tools and exercises I've shared with you so far in this book have you tried?

All of them?

Some of them?

Or maybe ... none of them? And if that's the case, do you feel bad, like you're not committed enough? Or do you feel guilty, because you think you're not doing what's expected of you?

Know this: I have no expectations of you. No demands, no standards for you to reach or goals you should meet. If you've wholeheartedly embraced practicing the tools, that's okay. If you haven't, *it's still okay.*

What I am interested in is what do you, dear reader, think

of your commitment to this book? And what if we go wider, to other areas of your life — what standards have you set for yourself? And, what happens when you don't meet those standards?

For instance, do you believe you get enough exercise? Eat enough vegetables? Are you always patient with your kids? Are you the partner you think you should be to your enjoyable other? Are you a great daughter / son / sister / brother / friend / coworker / neighbor? Are you super organized and dedicated to every task you take on?

Are you … perfect?

I'm going to guess you're not — and it's okay! I've met and worked with hundreds of thousands of people and I've never met a perfect one yet, and I'm pretty sure I never will. I'm including the man in the mirror, by the way. I like him a lot — but he's not perfect! Wait, let me rephrase that: I like him a lot — *and he's not perfect.*

Something I have found from working with people all over the world is a common belief among some that they should be perfect, or close to perfect — and when they're not (notice I didn't say "if they're not") they judge themselves harshly.

There are also a lot of folks who have very high expectations of others, and when those expectations aren't met, judgment comes out in full force to the extent that the person feels affronted and let down.

The thing about expecting perfection, or expecting anything concrete at all, is that it leaves little room for anything else to come into your life.

Think about how it is when you start a new relationship, or when you see your friends in that honeymoon stage after they've just met their current Mr. or Mrs. Right. Everything the new partner does, says and represents is *perfect*.

Here's where it gets messy: If you decide that someone is perfect, what happens when they do something that doesn't meet that idea of perfection? You were so focused on them doing what you think they should do that anything else looks like failure.

A judgment, by its very nature, solidifies a point of view, and nothing that doesn't match that point of view can come into your awareness. Pretty limiting, right?

> *How many positive judgments have you had of people just in the last three months that have stuck you because they haven't lived up to what you've judged them as being? Everything that is, will you destroy and uncreate it please?* ***Right and wrong, good and bad, POD & POC, all 9, shorts, boys and beyonds.***

I've said this already and I'll say it again: Judgment is a killer. It's a killer of possibilities, it's a killer of space, it's a killer of energy, it's a killer of joy, it's a killer of happiness.

Moreover, it's the number one cause of pain, suffering and illness on the planet. As a body whisperer, understanding more about judgment and its destructive and limiting nature puts you in a place where I believe hardly any other healers on the planet are right now, and a place where you can bring change into your own world and the world of the people you work on with real ease.

The thing about judgment is that it's an ingrained habit, and it's no one's fault that they picked it up. It's almost like a reflex. We've been conditioned to judge *everything* about us. Everything we think, everything we choose, everything we do is labeled as good or bad, right or wrong.

What if it didn't have to be that way?

What if it's not the way you really are, underneath all the conditioning? What if dropping judgment altogether would be like a homecoming, and a return to your true nature?

Almost like getting your wings back?

You had those wings when you were a baby, by the way. You didn't come into the world judging yourself or others; you were a little ball of conscious energy and light.

As with any habit, judgment is a habit you can choose to break.

In just a few pages, I'll be sharing a set of tools that you can use to let judgment go, but first I really want to drill down a little deeper into this concept of judgment, because there might be more to it than you're aware of right now.

A new lens on judgment

Going back to basics, we can say that judgment is the act of labeling a person, a thing, an event, a situation, a thought — anything at all — as good or bad, right or wrong.

When you choose consciousness, the polarities of good and bad no longer exist. Everything in your life loses those conclusive and limiting labels and becomes *interesting*.

Every choice you have ever made or will make, whether it's a choice that leads to bankruptcy or a choice that results in winning a million dollars, is just ... interesting.

How is that sitting with you?

We're used to hearing about how damaging negativity can be, but what about so-called positive points of view? Could winning a million dollars really just be interesting?!

As a seeker, by which I mean someone willing to look beyond the confines and limitations of this reality (I know you're a seeker because you're here, reading this book) you might have been trying to school yourself out of negative thinking and into positive thinking for a while. Maybe you've dabbled with affirmations and other techniques for cultivating a positive mindset and outlook. If that's the case, the idea that 'good' or 'positive' judgment is something to stop participating in might be a tough one to accept, but please — hear me out.

If we're going to let go of judgment, we need to make a commitment to doing it wholly and completely.

Why? Because if we keep on with the belief that some things, or people, or situations are 'good,' then by default we're saying some people and situations are 'bad.' It's the polarity thing again: In the polarities of this reality, good can't exist unless there is bad. Right can't exist unless something or someone is wrong.

Now, before we go any further with this, know that letting go of judgment doesn't mean we suddenly get really complacent about everything, and it doesn't mean that we allow people to do crappy things to us because we're so enlightened that we're just thrilled to lie down and let people walk all over us.

No. Instead, we tap into something so much more expansive than judgment: awareness.

Replacing judgment with awareness

Here's the thing: You can be *aware* of a negative situation or person who is intending to limit you, and not be in judgment of it or them.

And, you can be *aware* of a positive person or situation which is making your life greater, and again, not be in judgment of it or them.

The difference between an awareness and a judgment is that judgment has a point of view attached to it. Say for example you start exercising daily and you're feeling amazing. You judge this new behavior as good for you and the right thing to do. And then ... you don't work out one day, and that turns into two days, three, then a week. How do you feel? My guess is you feel like a failure.

How could you *not* feel like a failure when you decided that exercising made you a success?

It's completely possible to be aware that you feel good when you exercise regularly without judging that behavior as good, right, exemplary and so on. And, you can notice someone acting selfishly, or being mean, or rude, whatever it is — acknowledge it, see how limiting their behavior is, and still not judge them for it. You just acknowledge it, without charge, and without a point of view attached.

Once again: Letting go of judgment doesn't make you

a doormat or passive. In fact, when you stop seeing the world, and other people — and yourself — in a black and white way, you actually get a lot more in tune with what will create more in your life and what will create less. You stand in your power and potency in a way you never imagined you could. You allow for so much more growth, fun, joy and *healing* in your life.

Here are a couple of clearings to help you release any misconceptions you may have around positive and negative judgment.

> *Where have you decided that anything positive that you think must not be a judgment and anything negative you think must be a judgment, will you destroy and uncreate it please?* **Right and wrong, good and bad, POD & POC, all 9, shorts, boys and beyonds.**

> *How many things that you thought were negative did you have awareness of about people, like they're selfish, or they're unkind or they're stealing from someone? How many of those did you have as awarenesses that you thought were judgments that actually were not judgments, they were awarenesses, but you decided because it seemed negative it must be bad and wrong so you cut off your awareness of where the person was functioning and then you became the effect of them and where they're functioning? Everything that is, times a godzillion, will you destroy and uncreate it please?* **Right and wrong, good and bad, POD & POC, all 9, shorts, boys and beyonds.**

Is this lightening up for you? I've seen so many people get an immense sense of freedom when they glimpse what's possible when they let go of judgment. When nothing is good or bad, and only 'interesting,' their whole being gets brighter, and they know they're on the way to getting their wings back. It's no surprise, because judgment is a huge burden — metaphorically and physically.

The energy of judgment

Almost all disease, hurt and pain in people's bodies is based on a judgment — or several judgments — that they have around a situation. It might be their own judgment, or it might be something they've bought as true from someone else.

Here's how that works: As we've explored, the body uses the language of energy to try to communicate with us, and many of us, perhaps you included, have had a really hard time hearing this energy. The energy solidifies to try to get our attention until eventually it turns into something like a frozen shoulder *and then* — at last — we feel it, *and then* we have the audacity to say, "Wait! How did that happen?!"

We think the frozen shoulder came on suddenly, when in fact it could be the result of many years of accumulated energies, all of which originated in judgment.

Just think for a moment about the energy of judgment.

Think about those good, bad, right, wrong labels we affix to everything and everyone. Do you notice they have a heaviness, and a solidity? Kind of like concrete that's about to harden and solidify? That's the energy judgment has.

Now, let's get the energy of *interesting*. Imagine if something isn't good or bad, just interesting. In fact, let's call it *interesting point of view*. What's the energy of that?

The beauty of 'interesting point of view' is that it completely pulls the rug out from under judgment. It takes away its validity. We're going to look at it again in a few pages as a tool for letting go of judgment, but just for now, notice how much more space you get when you view a person or a situation or a choice as interesting.

Someone doesn't like you? *Interesting.*

That time you embarrassed yourself in front of someone you really admired? *Interesting.*

Someone thinks your taste in home decor is terrible? *Interesting.*

Doesn't *interesting* give you so much more space around a situation?

Interesting point of view doesn't solidify like judgment does; it has a totally different energy about it, and — here's the key: It won't create pain, hurt or disease in that beautiful body of yours.

Do you know you get more of what you direct your energy to?

Your body is kind of like an animal, or maybe a lump of clay. Wait! Don't throw the book across the room. Hear me out.

Your body — and mine! — is like an impressionable, sweet, lump of clay that's here saying to you, "I'll give you whatever you want — just tell me what that is. I'm ready!"

And what do we give our bodies? Judgment. We catch sight of ourselves in a mirror and we instantaneously throw a handful of judgments at our sweet, giving bodies. "Ugh, my butt is so saggy. And look at those crow's feet. Am I developing jowls? I've always hated my thighs, they're so fat…."

The heavy and intense energy of judgment gets taken in by our bodies and, eager to please and give us what it thinks we want, the body gives us a saggier butt, deeper crow's feet, heavier jowls and thicker thighs. We've directed that energy of judgment at our bodies with such intensity that the body absorbs it and says, "Oh that's what you want! No worries, I can do that for you."

> *How many judgments have you had of your body*
> *just in the last 24 hours? Everything that is, times*
> *a godzillion, will you destroy and uncreate it please?*
> **Right and wrong, good and bad, POD & POC, all**
> **9, shorts, boys and beyonds.**

Who or what creates your reality?

Some of us have this idea that our judgments and conclusions about the world are mere facts and reflections of the world. Some people truly believe that when they judge something as good or bad, they're just saying it as they see it.

My point of view is that nothing is as we judge it to be. It is our judgment which creates our reality. In essence, it's our point of view which creates our reality — not the other way around.

What if. . . .

Your point of view creates your reality; reality doesn't create your point of view.

That's a game-changing concept. Would you like it again?

Your point of view creates your reality; reality doesn't create your point of view.

Just think about it for a moment. Have you ever met someone whose outlook on life is really negative? They'll often lament that they're unlucky, tell you how often they're ill, and that things hardly ever work out for them. And then … they get a ton of bad luck, they catch every bug going and — surprise, surprise — things hardly ever work out for them.

What if their point of view is creating their reality? Could it really be that straightforward?

I believe it is. What do you think? If you can allow the concept that you're creating your world into your world, you're on track for incredible change.

Are you willing to undo any judgments you have in your body and your life … right now?

It's your willingness to let go of judgment that's the catalyst for life-changing greatness. When you make a judgment and aren't willing to change it, you keep whatever problem or limitation you have there, in place. While it's there, the only thing it can do is continue to create whatever havoc it's creating in your life. Aches, pains, sadness and suffering — you name it, it's there for the long haul — until it isn't. Until you choose something else.

When you're willing to let go of judgment, run the following clearing. I'll be sharing lots more tools for letting go of judgment in the next few pages, but this is a great starting point for you — and it's a great one to share with your clients.

> _All the judgments you have that are creating the havoc_
> _in your life and the havoc in your body that you believe_
> _you cannot change, will you destroy and uncreate it_
> _please?_ **Right and wrong, good and bad, POD &**
> **POC, all 9, shorts, boys and beyonds.**

Ready to let go of even more?

What would be possible then?

Getting out of judgment: A toolkit

First: STOP!

Here's where you make a commitment: From this point on, notice when you're judging yourself, and how often, on any given day. Just by casting your mind over the day so far, consider this: Have you judged yourself much yet? For some people judgment starts when they look in the bathroom mirror first thing in the morning; for others it starts before they even open their eyes.

Here's your mission. For the rest of the day, take notice of any judgmental thoughts that come to you, about you, and as soon as you notice these thoughts surfacing, simply tell yourself to STOP.

You don't have to explore it further, or wonder why it's happening, or get deep about it in any way — just give yourself the STOP command and continue on with your day.

I've shared this tool with so many people, and some tell me they like to imagine a hand, or a STOP sign, or something else visual; some say it out loud while others say it quietly to themselves. Do whatever works for you, the point is … to just do it! Here's the clearing to follow it up with:

Everything that is, and everywhere I bought that, I now destroy and uncreate it. **Right and wrong, good and bad, POD & POC, all 9, shorts, boys and beyonds.**

What if two seconds later you judge yourself again? Easy — you just tell yourself to STOP again, and use the clearing another two or ten or two hundred times if you like. The idea is to break the thought pattern, the habit, the cycle of judgment, even if it's just for a few seconds. By becoming aware of it, you get to control it, and then you can choose to do it less.

It's in awareness where your freedom is born.

The body is a great place to start practicing eliminating judgment, because, as we've discussed, we are so very prone to spewing a litany of judgment on our bodies.

If you'd like to take this further, ask yourself, *What are the top five areas of my body that I judge on a consistent basis?*

Then, whenever you notice yourself judging that part of your body, whether it's your hips, your arms, your stomach, your nose, your feet — see the hand or the STOP sign and run the clearing.

That's it! You don't need to work any harder than that,

because you don't *need* to work any harder than that for space to open up in your life where previously there was only constriction.

If you're willing, do this for the next three to five days— whatever you're comfortable with. See what happens. You might get the sense that this is actually more easily change-able than you ever thought it was.

Next level

Would you be willing to notice when you do 'good' judg-ment about your body too?

Not everyone is happy about undoing 'good' judgment, and I understand that because I know how hard it can be to feel good about yourself in this reality. If you don't feel comfortable using STOP and running the clearing on good judgment, it's enough to just notice when you do it for now, and perhaps ask this question: *What will it take for me to let go of every kind of judgment?*

Please remember, you can be aware you have beautiful hair, a defined torso, the softest lips, a truly caring nature, a wonderful sense of humor — you just don't have to attach judgment to those things. You don't need to give anything up. Choosing to use these tools, or anything I'm sharing with you, will never lead you to a place of less-than.

I say this often because it's true: You have nothing to lose — except your limitations.

Choose gratitude

If you're looking for an antidote to judgment you will *always* find it when you choose gratitude. Judgment simply cannot exist wherever there is gratitude. If you're grateful for your whole body, and every individual part of it, you'll find judging it really, really hard to do! When you get that sense of appreciation about the amazing things our bodies do for us and with us, it gets so hard to give it a hard time.

Simply: In any situation, you can either have gratitude or you can have judgment. The two don't co-exist. Whenever you choose gratitude, judgment goes away, and vice versa: If you choose judgment, gratitude goes away. It's hard to be grateful for something you think is not enough.

If you had to choose between judgment and gratitude, what would create the most for you and your body?

What are you choosing to be with your body right now?

Interesting point of view, I have this point of view

Going back to our conversation a few pages ago, we looked at how *interesting point of view* has such a different energy to it than judgment. Would you like to apply it in a really practical way to bring amazing change in just a few moments?

Think about any upset in your life from the last couple of weeks that's still present and bothering you. It might be about a person, or an event, a conversation, an altercation, anything at all that pushed your buttons. Get the energy of it, however uncomfortable it is.

Now say this, with the uncomfortable energy still present, "Interesting point of view, I have this point of view." Say it out loud or just to yourself, whatever you feel okay doing.

Interesting point of view, I have this point of view.

Notice what happens to that original energy you just conjured. Has it shifted a little? You might find that what was very heavy and restrictive a moment ago has lightened, even if it's just a tiny bit.

Now, do it again. To that new, lighter energy, say it again: *Interesting point of view, I have this point of view.*

Is it lighter still? Is there more space around it?

Keep doing it: *Interesting point of view, I have this point of view.*

You can do it as many times as you like, but I usually find that just three times completely changes the energy around it.

Warning: It can get addictive! And it's so simple.

What you're experiencing is the place of total freedom, the place beyond judgment.

The beautiful thing is you can use this for anything and everything in your life and it will obliterate the judgment around it. When you function from *interesting point of view*, there is no right and there is no wrong. Everything is just as it actually is.

For me, *interesting point of view* can feel like the embodiment of a huge sigh of relief. Peace descends, and I start to be a different space for people around me, including those I work on and with.

Consider this: Put yourself in the position of a client for a second. Would you rather go to a practitioner who has, *and is*, the energy of *interesting point of view*, or would you rather be in the presence of someone operating with and from judgment?

I know which I'd prefer, and I think it's the same for you too.

When you're a space of no judgment for someone, healing change is set in motion.

Think of somebody who doesn't judge you

Let me ask you a question, and it's one I've asked in classes around the world for the last 20 years.

Do you have somebody in your life who doesn't judge you and doesn't think you should be any different than you are right now?

Think about that person for just a moment. What is it like to be in their presence? Isn't it amazing?

If you don't have somebody like that in your life at the moment, I'm really sorry.

Could you be that person for yourself?

Could you be that person for the people who come to you?

It's when you choose to practice from *interesting point of view* and not from judgment that you find clients who are drawn to you. Believe me, you'll get more bookings and interest than you ever thought possible. Why? Because, whether they know it or not, being with someone who doesn't judge them is one of the main things people on this planet are searching for.

Who's the person in your life who you want to call when something goes wrong? Is it the one who tells you how bad your choices are, or the one who lets you talk, and after not long at all that weight of the world lifts from your shoulders?

That person is functioning from no judgment, with no expectations of you and no projections about who they think you should be.

What if you could be that for your clients?

You can — and you've made the move to start being that. Practice the tools in this chapter and you'll get really good at noticing when any kind of judgment comes into your world — and letting it go.

Another possibility

A lot of our focus so far has been on letting go of judging our bodies and ourselves, which is the most obvious place to start.

What if you were to widen your attention of this, and notice when you judge other people or their choices too?

At the time of writing, we're in an era of human history where a lot of citizens of the world are frustrated and angry with the politicians and policy makers who seem to rule the planet. As angry as you may be at certain political figures, if you really want to make a change in the world *and* step into your true power as a healer, the most effective step you can take is to let go of your judgments about those people.

Remember: Your judgment merely solidifies what is already there.

Until now you might have thought you only ever have two choices in responding to any event:

You can align and agree, which is the positive polarity,

Or,

You can resist and react, which is the negative polarity.

Now you have the awareness of a third option: You can be *interesting point of view* — the option with no polarity to it. You can view a situation and simply recognize what's going on. That is such a powerful place to be, and contrary to what a lot of people will tell you, it also happens to be the place where you create the most change.

Most of us have been taught that we have to fight against certain causes or injustices in order to affect change. We've been taught that unless we choose a side and take a stand against the wrongs we see in the world, nothing will change, and nothing can get greater. That's a lie. A big one.

The truth is that our potency lies in choosing to BE *interesting point of view (IPOV)* about those people, events and injustices that we wish to make greater. When we go beyond the need to fight and prove how wrong the other side is, we are much more likely to initiate change. Being IPOV is what allows us to open the space for possibilities to exist, and that's how we quite literally become a space of change. Fighting against a person or a cause is no longer required. BEING is all that is required.

And haven't you been fighting against limitation for long enough? Choose to be the space of IPOV and that different world you've been desiring will begin to actualize right in front of you.

IPOV is the platform where your healing rocket can take off. The closer you get to the space of being, the more change you can create — and you can do it faster and on a bigger scale than you ever thought possible.

PART
THREE

A NEW
WAY TO
HEAL

Is it time to take your new awarenesses
to the next level?

—

What if you understood even more about your
gift as a body whisperer?

—

What if you could initiate meteoric change in
people's lives, by being in allowance, by being
present with the energy of anything that ails
them, and by asking questions?

—

What if you could BE the question?

—

And what if you really knew and understood
the value of your gift — and you weren't afraid
to receive?

Stepping Away From Empathy, Sympathy And Devotion

Do you know what an empath is? Could you be one?

An empath is somebody who has the capacity to heal, so I'm willing to say anyone who's read this far into the book is an empath.

As an empath, you have the ability to create change in people's bodies and in their lives. The change you create can happen on a person-to-person basis *and* on a planetary level. You are that powerful, that caring, and that much of a gift.

Do you sense a 'however' coming up? It's a very friendly one!

Here's the thing about empaths — and this is not a criticism, just an observation from my years of working with so many ... and being one! In fact, what I'm about to share is part of the territory of being a body whisperer — and it's something I used to do too.

As we looked at in Chapter 4, in our efforts to help ease the pain and suffering of others, we have the capacity to take that pain and suffering on ourselves. We can do this with the people we care about, the clients we see, and even strangers we meet or pass by in the street.

Often, we do it without even being aware we're doing it: You might have a session with a client who has a physical complaint like a frozen shoulder, and not long afterward your own shoulder will start to ache. Their shoulder felt so much better, by the way — because you, in your effort to help, care and heal — took their pain and suffering into your own body.

It can happen with psychological symptoms too. Have you ever been around someone who's feeling depressed, and you notice a wave of sadness overwhelm you — just as they start to feel better? You took on their pain.

On the one hand, you're doing something amazing: You're healing people! Those who come to you for change are thrilled because you've given it to them — but on the flip side it's temporary change; their pain will come back.

Why? Because they didn't *choose* to give it up; *you took it away*. Even though you did it from a place of caring, the key element is that you were led by empathy, sympathy and devotion. And though you may never have realized it or played with this idea before, empathy, sympathy and devotion are all superior points of view. Why? Because they place you *above* the person you're working on.

When you empathize or sympathize with someone in pain, and you devote yourself to taking that pain away — you're making *you* the most powerful person in the interaction. You're the one with the cure, the antidote, the remedy, and the other person needs you in order to feel better.

Shining a light on the true nature of empathy, sympathy and devotion presents us with a totally different way of looking at healing, and it's not at all about making you wrong for practicing from empathy, sympathy or devotion. I know it stems from your caring — the thing is, I also know you are capable of so much more. And it really just comes down to this:

The gift of choice

Realize that your job — your gift as a body whisperer — is to empower people to make a different choice, and *that's* the key to their true healing. You, just by being you, allow them to become aware of a different possibility.

Now, the tools to assist you with that are coming to you in this chapter and throughout the book, but for now I'd just like you to start to recognize this because it is actually quite a radical point of view in healing — and it's one that allows for so much more change to occur: When you take on someone's pain or suffering, you're actually taking away their autonomy and power *to choose to let go of it themselves.*

Choice is the key to healing, and it's your clients' choice that unlocks the door to their greater, pain-free life.

I believe we're living in an era where we're required to empower people. And you, with your capacity to empower people to choose something different, are a rare and wonderful breed.

You've heard the age-old adage: If you give someone a fish they'll eat for a night, but if you teach them to fish, they can feed themselves for the rest of their days. This is what you're doing: empowering people to be well, to be happy, to be fulfilled for their entire lives — not just while you temporarily take their pain away.

And, here's the key: If you show someone that they have the power to choose to change whatever is going on for them — awesome. If they choose not to change it — still awesome.

This means you don't punish you, you don't chastise them, and you don't get mad at the world and give up on being a body whisperer because of the injustice and frustration of it all when someone doesn't choose consciousness and change.

It's not your responsibility to change people. Even when you have someone on your table who you care about and feel connected to, someone you totally get, someone you really, really want to help. Taking on their problem is not going to work — ever.

Your gift is to inspire people to choose change for themselves.

In short: It's not about you. I've seen so many gifted healers get stuck in a cycle of judgment when their clients don't choose to change. Honestly, I've seen it 100 times over. If this feels familiar at all, please run this:

> *Everything you've been doing to create the wrongness of you as a healer, the wrongness of you as somebody who facilitates change, and the wrongness of you as somebody who can't do it enough for enough people in a short enough amount of time to actually change the world in the way you know is possible, will you destroy and uncreate it please?* ***Right and wrong, good and bad, POD & POC, all 9, shorts, boys and beyonds.***

As frustrating as it can be when you know someone should be able to choose something and they choose not to, when you detach yourself from the emotion of it — *from the superiority of it* — you practice with so much more ease and effectiveness. You no longer have to devote yourself to getting others to change, and you no longer need to take their pain into your own body just to give them some relief.

All you have to do is show them a possibility beyond pain by your very being. And show them a possibility beyond suffering by allowing them to know it doesn't have to exist anymore.

Here's how: You BE the energy

Your gift is to be with your clients with no judgment, from a place of total caring, and to see the brilliance and beauty of them. Be there as a space of being that is totally vulnerable. Be willing to walk through any of the trials and travails they've had or are having. Be a source for a greater possibility, and support and nurture them to recognize that they have the power to choose.

This way of being with people creates a change unlike anything else I know. Things will shift in their life, their body, their world, their psyche and psychology that previously seemed impossible. And it all stems from you practicing away from empathy, sympathy and devotion, and instead choosing to be the awareness that they can overcome anything.

See those you work on as the greatness they aren't able to see in themselves. It's not about saying it in words — it's a space beyond words. Words, especially compliments, are so often rejected anyway. Instead, you *be* the energy of the awareness of how great they are. And, at the same time, you *be* the awareness of the energy of everything you yourself have overcome.

When you're the awareness of the energy of everything that is truly possible, you give your clients the power to shift and change their entire world. The shifts and changes you enable them to create are absolutely phenomenal — some would even call them miraculous.

CHAPTER

7

Healing With Chaos

When you think about how disease affects the body from a biological point of view, what images come to mind?

When you visualize an illness or virus taking hold of the organs, the bones, the cells, do you get the impression that the body is under attack in some way? That something unruly and anarchic is disrupting an ordered system?

If you do, it's because that's the general consensus, and it's the point of view held by the majority of professionals who practice medicine and study disease. We've picked up on that point of view to the extent that when we talk about the effects of a virus, or an infection, or a condition such as cancer, we often use language that conjures the sense that something chaotic is going on, and something is challenging the status quo and peacefulness of our bodies.

I bought into this point of view too: *Chaos is bad, order is good*. Those staple beliefs formed my understanding about the nature of disease for most of my adult life. In fact, it's only in the past five years that I've accessed the awareness that something else is going on, and I'm so glad to be sharing it with you because honestly — it's a game-changer.

I always assumed that because I was interested in consciousness and greater possibilities, it was my job to bring order to the chaos of this world. I had the idea that order is what brings peace, while chaos brings unrest, turmoil and destruction.

And then ... the veil was lifted, and I got a totally new awareness:

Chaos is a creative force which acts as a major catalyst for change. Chaos is where the freedom and the possibility lies.

Now, this awareness was a bit of brain-fry when it first came into my world. Have you noticed how things that challenge your beliefs often are? Then, when I began instituting it in my practice, it started changing everything.

So, how did it come into my world?

As it often does: with a question, or in this case — with a lot of questions. About five years ago I had a particular client and the energy with this person was so heavy. So, so heavy, and so, so solid. I just couldn't get him to a place where he could dissolve it, and I was frustrated.

I started asking, *I wonder what it would take to change this?*

This question, by the way, is a great tool for those people you work on who are having real difficulty changing. We'll revisit this question, and others, in a few chapters when we look more closely at the amazing change that questions can initiate with your clients.

I was talking the situation out with Gary, as we do, and sharing my frustrations. Among the questions we conjured were, *I wonder what it would take to change this? I wonder what I would have to ask this person? I wonder what they would have to get the awareness of?*

We already knew that everywhere a person couldn't change, whether it was a disease, whether it was depression, or a fixed point of view with money, a fixed point of view with relationships, a fixed point of view with anything in their lives — they had ordered their reality into existence to such a degree that it wasn't moveable anymore.

But it wasn't until we went beyond that awareness by asking, "If those are order, what would it take for change to occur?" and in a heartbeat we got one word:

Chaos.

It was so light.

It was so light I couldn't deny it, and it was so light I just started laughing. Well, giggling actually. I realized I'd spent a massive portion of my adult life trying to bring order to the world and people's bodies when chaos is the key ingredient which allows freedom and possibilities.

With that one awareness so much lightness came into my world and it shifted how I saw almost every client relationship I had at the time. (And many of my non-client relationships also.)

You know how once you start seeing things from a different place, you start seeing everywhere where this new awareness might apply? I could see that every client scenario where I'd been stuck and unable to contribute a change had its roots planted in order. And when I reflected on any change I'd ever created for clients up until this point, whether they were stuck and fixed physically, emotionally, financially, in their relationships, or in their bodies — it didn't matter — every time change was created, it was created by introducing chaos.

Chaos is creative

A lot of people misidentify chaos as havoc, which from my point of view isn't the same at all. Havoc is a destructive force that always creates *less* in people's worlds.

Chaos is a creative force for change that always creates *more* in people's worlds. It's a dynamic distinction, and one that can come as a huge eye-opener.

A couple of years ago, a hurricane hit my neighborhood and flooded my house with three feet of water. This hurricane was big, international news. According to a lot of news outlets, and the opinions of my neighbors and concerned friends and family members, this hurricane *brought total chaos*. It damaged homes, cut power lines, closed businesses.

For me, it definitely brought me a headache, and the clean-up and restoration required a lot of my attention and energy.

However, in the re-building *my house became greater.* I got to make changes I never would have considered if my hand hadn't been forced. I appreciated my home in a new and fresh light — and that's what happens with chaos: *It creates a space for change, even when at first, that change appears to be uninvited.* The thing about change is: *It's always invited.* And it's always regenerative and it always has momentum — just as chaos does.

As body whisperers, our job is to restore movement in the form of chaos into people's worlds.

To unpack another layer of this awareness, let's take a closer look at both order and chaos.

Close-up on order

Every judgment is order. Every thought, every feeling, every emotion, every fixed point of view. Every projection, every expectation, every separation and rejection. And when your projections and expectations are not met, and you judge yourself and others and the world at large: That's order, order, order.

For everything you judge, nothing that doesn't match that judgment can come into your awareness. When you judge something, you're only willing to see it as one thing, one solid, sturdy, heavy thing with no capacity to move or change.

It doesn't mean that something else beyond it doesn't exist, it means all you're willing to see is the thing that matches your judgment and matches the rightness of your judgment.

Any time you have to be right, you're doing order. Any time you've decided you're wrong, you're doing order. Any time you have to maintain the rightness of your point of view or the wrongness of your point of view — you're doing order.

What energy are you picking up around the concept of order, by the way? Are you getting a sense of heavy, or light? Is it solid, or spacious?

And what about chaos? When you step away from the idea that chaos is violent, or destructive, do you get more of a sense of possibility, space and freedom around it?

Close-up on chaos

The game-changer for me came when I realized that consciousness is actually chaos.

Chaos is consciousness in motion.

Take a moment to think about the natural world: the trees, the plants, the amazing networks of fungi under and over the forest floor. Think of moss, of grass, of the first shoots of a daffodil in spring. Mountain ranges, lakes, volcanoes, the sea. In your mind, conjure a sense of the natural world. Feel it in your body.

Does it have an intensity to it?

Does it have a chaos to it?

There is chaos in nature, and it co-exists with the smallest element of order possible. Chaos is necessary and essential to nature, only it's never overpowered or contained by order. We, as humans, are the ones with the tendency to over-order our natural chaos.

Animals function from the chaos of being able to continuously move and shift based on their changing environment. Again, order is present, and again it's a minimal amount compared to the chaos. The order holds their bodies together, just like the chaos of a tree, the ocean and a volcano is held together by a modicum of order.

Isn't it beautiful when you see it like this?

Look to the skies for more: the stars, planets and the dark energy that scientists admit they don't fully understand yet. The sun keeps creating its own energy continuously: It's a wonderful example of chaos held together by order.

What if you and your body were as chaotic as nature, as animals, as the sun?

And could that be a beautiful, electrifying thing?

The energy of being ... alive

I believe that chaos is your natural state. I'm certain that when you were a baby, or a little kid first discovering the world, you did it from a naturally chaotic state — either physically with heaps of energy to run, jump, play, touch, try and taste — or in the realm of your imagination where your curious nature played with ideas, stories and concepts, and asked a lot of questions.

What if we could be like that again? Chaos with just the right measure of order to keep us functioning on this beautiful planet.

That energy, that intensity of being alive, is an intensely chaotic energy — *and it's a conscious energy* — because little kids don't attach a point of view to anything.

Where did your chaos go?

As chaotic as we may naturally be, that chaos is housed, in this reality, in a body with a mind attached. It's still there, but it may have dimmed, and waned, and become muted by the ordered points of view that come in continuously from the world outside.

Most of us are now pretty much mostly solid with a few chaotic pockets. What's a chaotic pocket? Those moments where you feel like you truly have the joy of being you. You might laugh outrageously, feel giddy, or feel calm and centered — it's different for all of us. The common element is a beautiful sense of lightness and connectedness to who you truly are.

How is this feeling to you? Can you let yourself be a little chaotic?

> *Everything that doesn't allow you to be as chaotic as you truly are, because you decided it was wrong, and you were told it was wrong so you decided you'd never*

be it again, especially because you're a healer type of person who never wants to do anything bad to anybody and you decided that if you were chaotic it was bad rather than recognizing that your chaos may be the greatest gift you could give everyone you've ever known, everyone you've ever met and everyone you've ever worked on, everything that is, will you destroy and uncreate it please? **Right and wrong, good and bad, POD & POC, all 9, shorts, boys and beyonds.**

Where do you, as a body whisperer, come in?

There are tools, questions and suggestions for introducing chaos into your practice in the chapters that follow. Right now, I'd love for you to just get the energy of chaos and what it can create in you and in the people that you work with.

One of your greatest gifts as a body whisperer is to re-introduce chaos into systems that have been too highly ordered — after all, every disease process is based on order.

Order is the slowness that you perceive in the part of someone's body where they have pain, stiffness or disease. It's the slowness in people who are depressed or sad. It's the slowness that dominates when chaos, that natural flow and movement of energy, is absent.

When you re-introduce chaos to your healing space, the change you create isn't linear. It goes way beyond an A + B = C way of working with clients.

In chaos, one molecule of change can create an entire universe of possibilities. In chaos, one question can open up an awareness to a totally different world of what might be available.

Where order leads to the destruction of possibilities, chaos leads to the destruction of order *and* the increase of possibilities.

By re-introducing chaos to the places that have order, you see people's bodies start moving more freely. You see them get more flexible in their emotional capacities so they have more emotional fluidity. You see them start to have a sense of joy, a sense of lightness and a sense of freedom again.

Chaos is constant movement and constant flow with no fixed point of view, no judgment of right or wrong, good or bad, it's just a movement of energy.

Isn't that exciting? Isn't it liberating?

Here's to you, here's to chaos, here's to consciousness — and here's to the possibilities we, together, can create!

CHAPTER
8

Congruency

How many times have you had this experience, or something closely related to it? You see an acquaintance, not someone you know intimately, perhaps a co-worker, after a big occasion like Christmas or New Year, or when they've come back after a vacation to somewhere amazing like Hawaii, and you ask what kind of a time they had. They say, "Oh, it was wonderful," only you're not so sure that's the truth. Their words are saying one thing, while their energy is telling you a different story.

If you were to ask, "Did you *really* have a wonderful time?" they might look a little surprised, but they'll probably still keep going with the line and say, "I really did!"

If you're feeling curious (or a little mischievous) you might ask again, and this time you find that they waver — or even crumble altogether — and blurt out the truth: "No, it was awful! My brother brought his new girlfriend and she was *so rude* to me and no one said a thing, and my dad was unkind to the waiting staff, and I was so embarrassed, and you know what? I just do not fit into that family, and actually I feel really alone when I'm with them and...."

Ah — wow. And all it took was a couple of questions to scratch beneath the surface and you got to the truth beyond their words. I'm not suggesting you do this anytime you bump into a friend or an acquaintance, by the way — accepting a first answer is fine. I'm sure you've told people that things were okay with you when they weren't because at that moment you didn't want to get into an intense talk about family drama on your lunch break.

The point is that it demonstrates how frequently what we say *with words* isn't a match for what we're saying *with our energy*: So often these two ways of communicating just aren't congruent.

When it comes to working as a body whisperer, you'll find that very often people will come to you and *verbally* tell you why they've booked to see you, and what they'd like you to change for them, while *energetically* they're saying something else.

What makes it a little trickier is that our clients don't always know that what they're saying isn't what they're asking for, really. They're not purposefully misleading us or covering anything up, they just haven't got clarity yet on why they've really come to us.

On the surface it can appear that they have, and they might be there in front of us saying, "I'd like you to ease my shoulder pain," or "I need help with my confidence," or "I really want to build a better relationship with my mom." And, because you think that's the information you need, you see this as your green light, and you get to work on those issues.

And then … after the session you have this nagging sense that you didn't do all you could have done for this person, and you know they have that sense too. Although they leave feeling *somewhat* happy, *somewhat* lighter, deep down you know you facilitated about 50% of the change you could create for that person.

This is rocky territory for the body whisperer: Without the awareness that your client wasn't congruent with their ask, you go into the wrongness of you, when the truth is you just weren't able to treat their true ailment or meet their real request — because they hadn't recognized it themselves yet.

The thing is, a lot of people are out of tune with what they require because they've spent a lifetime building their desires around other people's desires, and buying other realities as their own. It can really muddy the water when you're working with someone who is essentially unaware that they're living behind a mask, out of touch with what they and their bodies need. They're blinkered by what they think they want, and it stands in the way of the far greater reality they could actually have.

Enter ... you!

Understand that the universe has an impeccable sense of timing. Consciousness has an impeccable sense of timing.

This person is on your table, at a particular day and a particular time, paying the fee you ask for and choosing to see you and no one else. There's somewhere you can take them, something you can offer, that no one else can. And that journey begins when you get them congruent with what they're asking of you.

Bear in mind that you may well be the first person to do this with them, and if you did nothing more than get them clear on what they're really asking for, that would be such a gift — because once they can see it, or perceive it, or know it — they can start to change their current situation and create something else. And that's why they're seeing you — because you have the capacity to *see* them.

One of the greatest causes of suffering on the planet right now is so many people are not truly seen. Being willing to explore someone's world means *getting into their world*, being with them, being present enough to say, "Hey, you know what? *I know* you know something else is possible. I know *I know* something else is possible. Let's do what we can to create it together."

How is this feeling to you? Is there a chance that a lack of client congruency has gotten in the way of what you can really do and create for someone? And if it has, have you ever misinterpreted that as a failing on your part?

> _Everything you've done to make you wrong based_
> _on that sticking point, based on not actually getting_
> _a client congruent with what they were asking for before_
> _you went to deliver it, will you destroy and uncreate it_
> _please?_ **Right and wrong, good and bad, POD &**
> **POC, all 9, shorts, boys and beyonds.**

I'm so glad to be able to share this awareness with you because, seriously, before I came to understand the importance of congruency, I'd tie myself up in knots wondering why certain clients weren't experiencing the level of change I so wanted to bring to them.

I'd think, _Well, this person has told me she'd like a better relationship with her mom and I've used every tool in my kit to help with that, and I know these tools have created change for hundreds of other people — so why isn't it changing for her?_

I started looking at: _What do I need to do? What do I need to be? And what do I need to change in order to give this client, and all of my clients, not only what they're asking for, but so much more?_

That's when I got the awareness that there are two things to consider when a client tells me what they'd like from our time together:

Are they willing to have what they're asking for?

And,

Is it the time for them to have what they're asking for?

I came to realize that whenever the content of a person's words doesn't match the energy I'm perceiving as they speak those words, the answer to both of those questions above will be No: They're either unwilling to have what they're asking for, or it isn't time for them to have what they think they're asking for. Also, what people *think* they are asking for, may not be what they are truly requesting.

With this new awareness I could see that even if my client wanted a better relationship with her mom in the long term, it wasn't what I was there to do with her in that moment. There and then, there were other wants and requirements to deal with first. This one simple change in my awareness meant that I could assist this client with why she was actually there, which led to her sensing that something had dynamically changed for her, even if it wasn't what she SAID she desired.

How do you know if and when a client is congruent with their ask?

You ask! But that's half of the picture. The key is in the perceiving. Let's take a closer look at that.

Ask ... and perceive

To find what a person is willing to have from you in your session, you ask them — and then you perceive the energy. Then you might need to ask again, and perceive again. And again.

While asking is the way in, perceiving the energy that's conjured from the ask is how you get to know whether what a person is saying is what they actually want and are ready for.

I understand this might sound a little intangible, especially if you're new to working with energy — so I'm going to get more specific soon and give you a few examples of how this works for me.

First, let me try to put it into words what it's like when a client's words *do* match the energy.

There's a clicking into place. An *a-ha* feeling. Imagine two musical notes being played that are off-key, that just do not go together, that don't harmonize. Total discord. They jar.

And then ... when two notes are played that complement each other, they create something else entirely, and it makes sense, it feels right — *it's harmonious.*

That's congruency — and that's how it is when the energy matches the ask.

For me, the energy I'm perceiving expands. There's a lightness and I get the sense that I can dive in and start working now. It's an exciting and uplifting moment — it's like the universe has fired the starting piston and said, "Okay, go, Dain, go!"

The beauty of an open question

To get that harmony, that congruency, as close to the start of your session as possible, I recommend you start by asking your clients an open question — in other words, one that allows more than a simple Yes or No answer.

Even if you saw your client last week and helped ease their lower back pain, if you start with, "So, are we working on the lower back pain again?" you're starting with a closed question and it's only giving them a chance to say Yes or No, and it's most likely they'll say Yes. What they really require or want from you in this session might be totally different to what they required in the last session.

Open questions such as, "What are we working on today?" Or even just, "So, how are you doing?" give your client a chance to open up and share more with you right at the start of your time together. What comes out of their mouth still might not be congruent with why they're there with you — but in starting a dialogue you're in a place where you can start to navigate toward why they're here.

Personally, I use, "If you could have anything out of this, what would it be?"

Gary begins with a simple, "So, what's up?" which is a great way to get a person talking about what's going on in their life, and this leads him to an awareness of what they might like.

Phrase your question in whatever way works for you; play around and see what you get. Your job is to ask and perceive — and see their world start opening up as you guide them to what might be possible.

In practice: Ask and perceive

Let me walk you through an example of how ask and perceive works for me. We'll continue with the example from a few pages ago: the lady who tells me she'd like a better relationship with her mom.

At the start of our time together, I ask, "If you could have anything out of this, what would it be?" and she says, "I want a better relationship with my mom."

Now, while verbally she's saying that, energetically I'm getting very little. I'm perceiving the energy and nothing is expanding. Nothing is light and there's very little movement.

This is my clue that this isn't why she's seeing me on this particular day. While a better relationship with her mom might be something she desires, it's not what I'm here to work on with her today. Either she's not willing to have that improved relationship yet, or it's not time for her to have it yet.

I ask, "What else?" and she says, "Well, I'd like to change my money situation." And again, the energy I'm perceiving is still restricted; the space is small.

I ask, "What else?" and this time it's like a key turns in the door and she says, "You know what? What I would really like to be is *free*. I want to be free of all needs and all limitations and the idea that getting the approval of someone else is going to make my life work. I'd like to know I can do it myself."

Suddenly the energy goes from a grain of sand to a whole cosmos — and boom — I know I'm hitting something that I can actually facilitate. We've struck gold and now there's something I uniquely can gift to her, and that's when the session starts and I do my thing.

My work is energetic; yours might not be. But if you begin with the act of asking questions to get your clients to a place where they're willing to uncover *why* they're there with you, you're creating an immediate change in their reality by opening them up to what's truly possible before you even start working on them.

Your universe interacts with theirs and a change occurs that will probably surprise you and blow *your* mind as well as theirs.

Be mindful that most people come to you to create a change based on the most limited version of what they think they can have. They don't realize that they're living in a limited world when they could live in an infinite world — and you get to guide them there. You pop the bubble on the reduced reality they've bought.

I find this concept so inspiring because reaching congruency really is as easy as being present with your clients, asking what they would like, perceiving that, and then asking, *What else?*

You'll start creating so much more for the people you work on — and that makes your job so much more fulfilling.

From that expanded and fulfilled place, you might ask: *What else is possible in my sessions? How much more fun can I have? How much more change can I create?*

And how much lighter and easier can it be for me and everybody who comes to me?

Being In The Question

The act of asking a question is such a simple, beautiful gateway to change. From asking questions we're able to perceive energy, as we just explored in the previous chapter, and we're able to open the door to letting more chaos — continuous, glorious, healing change-making chaos — into our lives.

Now we're going to look at how much more effective we can be when we *be the question*.

One of the fundamental things you can have in your awareness as a healer is to continuously stay in the question. And not just when you're working on someone — but in every moment of your life.

If this concept of *being in the question* is new to you, please don't try to wrap your head around it. Read on, allow your curiosity to carry you, see what feels light to you, and see what you discover.

Here's the thing: Asking a question, or being in the question, or simply *being the question itself* is one of the quickest routes we can take toward change, for ourselves and for the people we work with.

A question allows us to get to the heart, or the crux, of any situation in a flash. Questions break down walls, let light and space in — *they let chaos in* — and they allow us to see what's keeping us stuck. From there we can undo and uncreate anything that's limiting us, *and* we can also access the possibilities for change to make our lives infinitely greater.

Being in the question is a key element of consciousness, and consciousness is all about choice. What else presents you with choice more than a question?

When you recognize you have choice it's incredibly liberating, whether you're realizing it for the first time or the thousandth time. Having choice means you're not at the mercy of anyone or anything else. You're in control of your life and your living, and it's such a beautiful place to be.

Questions are empowering, while answers are disempowering. Answers are conclusive, like a full stop, a period, a closed door. The issue is that answers are sought-after the world over. And the tricky thing is that usually, answers are exactly what our clients want from us.

Trickier still is that giving answers is often the instinct of a body whisperer: We want to help, and in our efforts to help we might have a tendency to assess a situation and make decisions with too much haste. For instance, we might get the sense early in a session that our client has an anger issue, and so we set about treating it with whatever techniques we favor and practice.

Now, our assessment could be valid — but what if it's not? What if we've made an assumption, and however educated and rooted in our training and our experience that assumption is, what if there's actually something else going on for that person, which is not available to us because we're not being with them from the space which questions allow?

And even if we *are* correct about the underlying anger issue, now might not be the time or the session to address it. Whether we're picking up on the truth or not, whenever we jump in and start healing without *being the question* first, we get the same result: frustration and a lack of forward movement for our client and for ourselves. At best our technique might bring temporary relief, much like hammering a screw into a piece of wood might work for a short while — even though what the screw needs is a screwdriver, not a hammer.

Something to note here is that in offering our clients answers, we're back in the territory of empathy, sympathy and devotion that we discussed in Chapter 6. Our aim, *our gift*, is all about offering choice, and answers do not offer choice.

Think about it this way: So much of what ails our clients is the result of the judgments and conclusions they've taken on. Their energy is blocked and solid, and they're often in great pain. How can we best heal them? By bringing more solidity into their bodies and their world via judgment and conclusion? Or by contributing space, possibility and openness to their bodies and their world, via questions, possibility and choice?

If there's one thing that has trapped more healers than any other, this is it: giving our clients *our interpretation* of what's going on with them, rather than asking questions so they come to *their own awarenesses* about what's going on with them.

When you give answers, and especially if those answers make your client's life greater, you become the source of that greatness. They will see you as insightful and perceptive, and they'll come to you for more answers. How empowering is this for your clients? Not very. In fact, not at all.

And what if your answer, based on your awareness, is even just 1% off-track? You'll burden your client with a lie, and that lie might stay with them for a very long time.

When we ask questions, we allow our clients to find their own answers. We give them the gift of their own greater awareness, and this is a gift that truly sets them free. Even better, it lasts for the rest of their lives.

Asking questions creates more space, more freedom, more joy and more chaos. It's how we create more of a healing change and it's what marks us —YOU — out as a body whisperer.

Questions and chaos

Chaos: That catalyst for change is all about movement, momentum and flow — and what better way to keep momentum going than to ask questions, and *be* the question?

When you step away from providing answers, cures and solutions, you can practice from a much more open place. Note the difference between:

"Hello. I'm going to assess you to find out what's wrong with you, and then I'll prescribe the reason I think this is happening and also the cure."

Versus:

"Hello. I'm here to be the question that allows you to unlock what's really going on for you. It may not be what you're expecting, and it might be unlike anything anybody has ever found before, but I can offer you the tools to unlock that door and create phenomenal healing and change."

Which approach allows more, and creates more?

How — and why — being in the question works

When we're in the question, we're able to perceive the solid energies of judgment and conclusion, as well as all the thoughts, feelings and emotions that are stuck in our clients' worlds. It's the way we tap into what's really creating problems in their body and their general well-being.

We can only perceive those solid energies when we don't have solidity in *our* world, and we do that by being in the question. We do that when we're in a place where we have nothing to prove, no need to be right, and no sense that we're wrong. We do it when we've let go of all need to give answers or provide cures or prove to our clients and the whole world that we're a good person because somewhere in us we think we're a bad person. . . .

... Did I go off on a tangent there, or did that speak to you? It's a common body whisperer hang-up: the need to prove we're good enough. If you got a flicker of something when you read that paragraph above, please run this:

> *Everything that brought up, and everywhere you feel the need to prove to you and the world that you are not wrong, will you destroy and uncreate it please?* **Right and wrong, good and bad, POD & POC, all 9, shorts, boys and beyonds.**

And please, please recognize that YOU ARE GOOD ENOUGH, and that your worth is not connected to how many people you help or cure or write prescriptions for.

In practice: Look for the chinks of light

When you're in the question you perceive energy so quickly and effectively. Your senses are heightened. You're alert, in an easy and peaceful way, and from this place your ability to perceive what's really going on with your client is amplified to a phenomenal level.

Here's how it can work. Usually, your client will say something, and you'll notice it has a little flash of energy to it, like a little *tink*, or a *chink*, or a *ping* of energy — however it shows up for you. It might seem like a bell ringing, saying, "Hello — this is important!" or it might be more visual, like a flash of light that gets your attention.

You might perceive this chink of light when your client is in mid-story, and you'll suddenly get a sense of: THAT! *That's what I need to know for now.* They're still going, still talking — but you've heard, or perceived, something beyond words. Energy is your first language, remember — and it's all you require.

What you're perceiving is where they're sticking themselves energetically. Listening for the chinks of sound or flashes of light (or something else you can't put a label on) is how you start to get the awareness of what's solidifying a person's body, brought on by the points of view that they've taken or bought as their own. If you can address and change those solidities, you can bring their body back to the chaos it naturally is, and where they can be healthy and happy from.

In the coming chapters we'll build more on this notion of being in the question and I'll offer you some tools to get you to that place, as well as some tools for moving through anything that seems to keep you stuck and unable to create the change you know you can. Right now, I really just want to share another reason why I have this point of view that being in the question is an awesome way to be....

It's so much more fun for you!

When you function from a place where your only aim is to provide answers you literally heal by numbers: You take Step 1, then 2, then 3, then 4, then ... you yawn, yawn, yawn! After a while, you feel like a robot and you get bored with your practice and your clients. Mostly that boredom and frustration stems from the fact that you're not creating the change you came here to create.

When you're a question, every moment of every day allows you to explore new possibilities with your clients — and that is just so much more fun, dynamic and fulfilling. AND SO MUCH MORE *YOU!*

Creating-as-you-go

Did you know the genesis of this book was actually a video series? When I set out to make Video Number One, I knew I had about 8000 tools that I could share — but who'd want to watch 8000 videos?

I did the same thing that I'm talking about right now: I functioned as and from the question as I made the series. I tapped into the energy of everyone who'd be watching, and although I knew there were some basic and fundamental tools and insights I wanted to share, I let it flow organically, just loosely based on what I have in my toolbox and what I know.

In that way, the video series was crafted as I went along, and it created so much more than if I'd written a detailed plan of everything I had to say to make sure my audience got all the answers they were looking for.

What if you did the same thing within your sessions?

What if each piece of information your clients gave you acted as a new awareness of where to go next?

Being in the question is how I operate at every level of my life. Any tool I've ever created, any change I've ever initiated, any class I've run, series I've made, book I've written — has occurred when I've been in the question.

Asking questions is the key to creating change, because change doesn't happen from a place of solidity.

If this idea of create-as-you-go feels light and exciting to you, you might want to consider: *How can I be the question more and more in my life?*

Get the sense of the ease and fluidity and possibility that every moment could present and be.

Where could *being the question* take you? What if being the question allows you to access inconceivable, unimaginable, indescribable experiences and things you can't even picture right now?

Isn't that electrifying?

BRINGING IT ALL TOGETHER

Practicing From Presence

Before we venture further, let's take a moment to look at some of the awarenesses and choices that may have opened up to you so far. Please note this is not a checklist to judge yourself against — it's more like a list of possibilities.

So far ...

... You may be developing a communion with YOUR body, learning to ask what it requires, and understanding that it has unique capacities as a psychic receiver.

... You might have lifted the veil on judgment, come to realize how destructive it is, and started to choose something far greater: to be with your own body and others from a state of allowance.

... You could be understanding more and more that your gift as a healer is to introduce choice into people's worlds: And your new awarenesses around chaos and being in the question are guiding you on how you can do this.

In this coming chapter, we'll build on some of the above by going a little deeper into how you *be* with your clients, as well as how to introduce more chaos into your sessions, and we'll look at how to tap further into your body's natural (and oh-so-useful) capacities as a psychic receiver.

Being with your clients

How are you doing with the idea of stepping into a space of being? If you've been working in this way for a while you might be totally at ease with it, or it might seem a little vague or out of reach. It may also push your buttons if you see yourself as a problem solver or someone who likes to *do*.

Please know that creating a space of being with your clients is still very much an active way of initiating change — and in fact, it's one of the most effective methods I know.

Being with a client is kind of like the bedrock or undercurrent of how you practice as a body whisperer. Even just thinking of that word 'whisperer' you get a sense of the gentle and easy nature of your gift, and the peace you can operate from. While it's true that your sessions and the work you do can get powerful and intense, it's your capacity to let go of judgment, and just be with the people you work on, that allows you to do your thing and create incredible change.

Perhaps the easiest way for me to tell you how I *be* with a client is to just tell you, as much as I can now, in words, on paper — and you can see if it opens something up for you.

In Chapter 6, I introduced this whole idea of *being* with your client as an antidote to trying to prescribe, solve and cure. Here's how I put it back there:

Your gift is to be with your clients with no judgment, from a place of total caring, and to see the brilliance and beauty of them. Be there as a space of being that is totally vulnerable. Be willing to walk through any of the trials and travails they've had or are having.

Be a source for a greater possibility, and support and nurture them to recognize that they have the power to choose.

Now let me tell you a little more.

In practice: How I just ... BE with a person

First, I push down all my walls and barriers. I lower every single wall in my world. This lowering of barriers is how I get to that space of being that's totally vulnerable.

I dissolve any and all resistance and reaction, as well as every alignment and agreement. I'm in a state of allowance and far, far away from judgment.

And I just ... be with my client in that clear, pure and sharp space.

Energetically, I take their hand and I say, *My brother, my sister, I am here for you and I am here with you. Whatever happens, I'm with you through this.*

And I just be with them,

and be with them,

and be with them.

I perceive what's going on in their world — while knowing that whatever I pick up there is not mine. I perceive it, I don't feel it. I don't take it on. In that way, as close as I am to them, you could say there's a modicum of distance too: And it's the distance that allows you to perceive from a more neutral space, which is where your power lies. You function like a fair witness, an impartial observer, and your strength comes from the fact you're choosing not to get involved in whatever is going on for your client.

This gives you the power to be what you perceive. You're there, you're tuned in, and you know and understand what's going on their world — but you're not taking it on as yours, and you're not in a superior position of *I Will Heal You*.

You take your client by the hand energetically and together you move forward. Think of a time when you would have appreciated this level of side-by-side companionship. I know there were times in my past when the care and presence of someone who could be there for me without judgment would have been life-changing. Being with your client in this way communicates that you're prepared to walk through anything with them: pain, fear, doubt, demons. You know that together you can get through this.

Alone — maybe not. Together — it's possible.

And you be with them,

and you be with them,

and you be with them.

You don't flinch. You know you're not wrong, and you

know whatever you're perceiving is not yours. You have their back, and even if you doubt you can help them — you choose to try.

Suddenly, that thing that troubled them, the thing that looked so terrible and vicious, the thing that they were sure would be the death of them — it dissolves.

Together, you've walked through the world filled with the demons of what they couldn't do and couldn't be. Together, by being present, by not buying their demons and pain as yours, by seeing the person as the gift that they are — you've started dissolving all of it.

If you choose to do this *and be this* for the people you work on, you can initiate a phenomenal shift in their world. Never again will they make themselves small in the face of those fears, pains and doubts.

And then, when you're on the other side, you talk to them: Talk about a change in their body, a change in their psyche, a change in their level of peace, of joy, of possibilities. You talk about a change in what they know they can accomplish in the world now.

You've guided them through facing their greatest fear, and you being in allowance *with them and for them* is what walks them through it, and now they know their greatest fear can never destroy, kill or limit them in any way.

You just empowered them to have a different reality.

Isn't that amazing? Isn't that why you are here?

Chaos In Practice

Chaos: that infinite, constant movement of energy. It's pure consciousness in motion.

Order: the solidity of energy. The solidity of any point of view that appears unchangeable and results in pain, stiffness and disease.

Gratefully, we now have the liberating awareness that chaos has the capacity to change those ordered, fixed, or stuck points of view and free our clients — and us — from pain and limitation.

You know you're that brilliant, right?

> *Everything that doesn't allow you to know that you*
> *have that awareness, that you have that consciousness,*
> *that you have that possibility, and that you have that*
> *level of brilliance that will allow you to not have to buy*
> *somebody's fixed point of view about what's going on,*
> *because remember, a fixed point of view is an ordered*
> *point of view, everything that doesn't allow you to*
> *have the awareness that you don't have to buy their*

fixed point of view, that you can actually go to a point of view of chaos which is — how can I change this with the most ease — will you destroy and uncreate it please? **Right and wrong, good and bad, POD & POC, all 9, shorts, boys and beyonds.**

How do we introduce chaos to those ordered systems?

We ask questions.

When you ask a question, you introduce a series of different possibilities into an ordered reality.

Even in what might seem like the small act of starting your sessions with an open question to seek congruency, you're introducing a little chaos right away.

A question always empowers and creates different possibilities. An answer always disempowers and creates fewer possibilities. Answers are what created the problem in the first place, of course. In an answer, there's a sense of *Conclusion reached: The End*. I know you understand there's more to life and consciousness than that.

When working on a client, you might ask yourself:

What chaos can my body and I be to change this in their body and their reality?

And another great question that's one of my favorites: *What are the infinite possibilities for this session?*

Asking questions allows you to open up doorways that didn't appear to exist before, and this invites that chaos into people's worlds — along with the healing, transformation, joy and possibilities which go way beyond the ordered dysfunction they're functioning from.

So many people try to order their choices into existence. Pretty much everything you'll work with as an energetic facilitator will stem from people trying to order their choices into existence.

They don't cognitively remember doing it, they have no idea how to change it, and they don't think there's something else possible.

You show them the way. You be that space of being with them, with no judgment, allowing them to access all the possibilities of chaos.

You be with them in such a way that they start to get an awareness of what they've chosen. They get the awareness that they've chosen it for a particular result. You be there with them in such a way that they get the awareness that there may be a different choice available to them.

In a sense, as you be with them, you communicate this: *You don't have to carry that heavy load of order around with you anymore.* And once they acknowledge that, you ask, *What would be a chaotic possibility that might bring something different into your world?*

In chaos, one element of change introduced into an ordered system can create a billion elements of possibility.

Chaos is continuous movement to greater possibilities. What the world requires right now is people who know that there's a possibility beyond solidity and into continuous movement.

People like you, dear reader, dear healer.

Your body functions from chaos: An example from Western medicine

A while ago, a female friend of mine had some health problems which resulted in her having to decide whether or not to have her uterus removed. She's familiar with Access Consciousness and she'd already used some of the tools I'm sharing with you in this book to assist her healing journey.

Are you thinking that she shouldn't have needed the surgery because she has access to all of these world-shifting tools? Or that I'd be able to cure her illness by working on her?

Well — I did work on her — and I did something chaotic. I asked for her body's point of view on the surgery. *Body, I said, Do you need the surgery? Will this help you or will it hurt you?*

I got a clear response: *I want the surgery, I need the surgery, this is what I require at this moment to assist me in what I can't do myself.*

When I relayed this to my friend, she said she'd asked her body too and had the same awareness. She was still a little hesitant, understandably, and wondered if we should be able to change her condition just with consciousness and Access tools.

Now, my response was that, sure — maybe we should, or maybe we shouldn't, but that's not where we were at right in that moment. I said, "Right now, given the conditions in these ten seconds in your life, your body apparently wants to have the surgery."

Again, she got the same awareness, and so she made the decision to have the surgery. Afterward, her tummy had a kind of indentation, and she asked her doctor if there was anything that could be done for that.

Her doctor's reply was wonderful: "Let your body handle it. Your body functions from chaos and it will re-organize itself in exactly the way it needs to. Your body knows what it's doing. We just helped it."

Now that's an awesome doctor.

Conversations with terminal patients

I'd like to take a moment to talk about cancer, because when you're on the frontline of working with illness, it comes up a lot, and it can be really intense — especially when the person you're working on has been given a terminal diagnosis.

These cases can seem difficult to navigate because they tap into your naturally caring nature, and your desire to help those bodies who are in pain. Terminal diagnoses are rocky terrain for the body whisperer, which is exactly the reason why I want to have this conversation.

First, I have to say: Please don't promise a client that you can heal their disease, or any disease for that matter. If you would like to offer some words, you can say you may be able to create a change that allows different choices to become available to them.

Cancer is actually order — although doctors will tell you it's chaos. Cancer is the result of a very highly ordered point of view that replicates itself in the patient's physical and physiological reality.

I'd like to share with you the question I ask any of my clients who have a terminal diagnosis. You might want to try it if it feels like it could work for you.

Here it is:

What are you dying to get out of?

Now, this question will almost always elicit a strong reaction. It's really unlikely anyone has asked your client this question before, and it's really unlikely their thoughts have ever turned in that direction — at least not in a way they can be aware of. Asking a question like, *What are you dying to get out of?* almost always gets an answer or a statement like, "I want to live."

When this happens, I accept what the client has said, and I'll add, <u>*"Everything that doesn't allow that, will you destroy and uncreate it please?* **Right and wrong, good and bad, POD & POC, all 9, shorts, boys and beyonds."**</u>

In other words: I POD & POC it.

Then I ask again, "What are you dying to get out of?" and they tell me again — they want to live. And I POD & POC that.

Then I ask again, "What are you dying to get out of?" and this time they might say something slightly different, and I POD & POC that.

Perhaps five, ten, fifteen, twenty-five layers later something will happen: A shift will occur. It might sound something like, "Oh my God, I'm dying to get out of my relationship."

Now this is excellent for me and for them — because at last we have the truth, and the awareness is out in the open. Oftentimes, the person doesn't actually want to uncover or acknowledge that kind of awareness; it's too difficult and painful to face. I mean — it had to be; they created a terminal disease to avoid it.

But here's the thing: That one awareness of the fact that they're creating this to get out of something that they don't think they have a choice for, *that's the introduction of chaos to an ordered system.*

That single awareness allows them to finally come out of the order, because the order tells them that's the only choice they have. I've never seen a physical problem that did not have a point of view attached; I've never seen a physical problem that was just a physical problem.

The awareness your client had as a result of you introducing an element of chaos (via your question) might sound something like, "I felt so stuck that I was actually willing to die to get out of my relationship when I could just ... get out of my relationship." That's chaos in the system. Then maybe, maybe, maybe — if they're willing — something can finally change, and the illness or disease process might change.

Again, I have to emphasize, any change that occurs is based on their choice. I would never claim to heal anyone. I would only claim to give people the awareness that they can make different choices for their body and their future.

Tapping Further Into Your Body As A Psychic Receiver

In Chapter 4: The Body As A Psychic Receiver, we looked at the concept that your body has the capacity to pick up on other people's pain and also their thoughts, and how recognizing and getting tuned into this not only makes your own life so much easier but it also places you at the leading edge of what you do as a body whisperer.

We looked at using this awareness on ourselves with the tool, *"Who Does This Belong To?"* and now I'd really like to share with you how we can use this tool to enhance the way we practice as healers.

Why *Who Does This Belong To?* is so relevant for you as a body whisperer

Acknowledging that the body takes on the pain and suffering of others is a huge game-changer for anyone working on people's bodies.

How many healers across the planet have access to this kind of awareness? And if they do — how many have the tools to go further and actually do something about it?

There are a few things to consider here:

- *Who Does This Belong To? is an awareness you can share with your clients so they can use it on themselves if they choose.*

- *It's a tool you can use as you work on them — more on that in a moment.*

- *It's also a tool which is especially useful for you, as a healer, to use on YOU: It enables you to keep your capacity to take on other people's pain and suffering in check.*

What do I mean by that last point? As a healer, practicing or not – your body is continuously trying to heal the bodies around it — so it stands to reason that your body has been taking on a lot of stuff from other people for a lot of years. If you're frequently exposed to the energies of pain and suffering on a daily basis, you might have been taking some of that on without even realizing it.

As a healer, you're acutely aware of the energies of what your clients present, and you feel it in your own body. To help you with that, I'd like to share a really useful clearing for all of you who work with other people's bodies, and it's one I suggest you run every day.

How many of your clients' problems have you locked into your body as a way of trying to heal it and take it away? Who does that belong to? Everything you did to buy it as yours, everything you did to lock it into your body as yours, and everything that doesn't allow you to let it go and recognize they won't take it back, you've already taken it away, will you destroy and uncreate it please? **Right and wrong, good and bad, POD & POC, all 9, shorts, boys and beyonds.**

You could say that your capacity to take on pain *and heal it* is both a gift and a curse, but it only becomes a curse if you don't acknowledge that it can happen, or if you don't want to believe it can happen, or if it's too weird for you that that can happen, or if you're not willing to use this tool with your clients.

Let's look at that next.

Using *Who Does This Belong To?* with your clients

There are several ways you can use this question when working on someone's body.

First, you can offer a client the awareness that their pain might not actually be theirs at all by sharing those two insights that I gave you back in Chapter 4:

Between 50 and 100% of what goes on in your physical body may not even be yours, and 98% of what goes on in your mind doesn't belong to you.

Now, as I'm sure you know, not everyone on the planet is ready for that kind of information, so use your own discretion when it comes to deciding who will receive this information and be open to acknowledging it.

A really simple way of introducing it in a session is just by asking the question:

Who does this shoulder pain belong to?

Who does this sadness belong to?

Then see how your client responds. True, you might receive a confused look, and you can choose to go along with that if it suits the situation, maybe by saying, "Well, I've been reading this weird book, and it said that somewhere between 50 and 100% of what goes on in our bodies actually doesn't belong to us. We can actually take things on from other people; how interesting is that? Would you like to just play with the possibility of it and see where it takes us?"

If you have already chosen to use this tool on your own body, you could also share how it's worked for you, and relate any changes you've noticed as a result.

Your principle aim is just to offer them the awareness.

If they accept it you might find they suddenly understand where their pain is coming from, and if that happens you can say: "Everything you did to lock that into your body, everything you did to take it on as yours or buy it as yours when it wasn't, will you let that go now please?"

When they say, "Yes," you can run the clearing statement out loud, or under your breath, or silently — it's up to you. "Right and wrong, good and bad, POD & POC, all 9, shorts, boys and beyonds."

Personally, I say it out loud because all of my clients know this is how I work, but as I've said before, saying it under your breath or silently works just fine.

In practice: *Who Does This Belong To?*

I'd like to share a story of how I introduced this question to a client when I first discovered it.

Back when I was still a practicing chiropractor, I had a patient with excruciating back pain, and I'd been treating him for several months without creating any long-lasting change.

Each week this guy came into my practice with pain he described as an eight out of ten on the pain scale. I'd work on him for an hour and the pain would go down to a two or a three, but he'd always come back the following week with the pain back to an eight.

It was incredibly frustrating to the point where I recommended he try another chiropractor because I just couldn't create the results that he needed, but he was adamant that he keep coming to me. Even though I could only get him out of pain for a short amount of time, it was the only relief he could get and he needed it.

This was around the time that I started going to Access classes, where I was picking up and learning the kind of tools I'm sharing with you now. When one particular week I was introduced to this very tool, *Who Does This Belong To?* I instantly thought — *I'm going to try this with my Excruciating Back Pain Guy.*

When he next came into my office it took him about five minutes to relax enough to get on to my table and lie down. Once he was as settled as he could be, I said, "Hey, I've got a weird question: Who does this back pain belong to?"

He pushed himself up, looked over at me and said, "My wife!"

Now, this was a guy who could barely move a moment ago, and there he was, propped up, looking at me like all the pieces of a puzzle had just fallen into place.

It transpired that earlier in the year his wife had hurt her back really badly and had been in terrible and continual pain for months. She'd had surgery and it had only worsened her condition. This man had seen what his wife was going through, and his caring for her was so great that he'd thought to himself: *I'll do anything to take this pain away from the woman I love so much.*

His body was listening dutifully and it took note, and within two weeks his wife's pain started to decrease, and four weeks after that — he started having back pain, which worsened and worsened, and no doctor could find the cause.

Once he'd relayed this to me, I told him about the new awareness I'd just got that week: Our bodies will try to heal each other if they can, and we have the capacity to take pain away from people and lock it into our own body as a means of healing them. I added that we're especially good at that when the person in pain is someone we care about.

This awareness resonated so much with him that in the hour that followed we got him out of 98% of his pain, and this time the results were long-term. He still has a small twitch that won't completely go away, but his entire life has changed, and all from the application of this tool: *Who Does This Belong To?*

The essential piece of information here is this: If some-body has bought something as theirs, if they have taken on the pain or suffering for somebody else, *they can't change it or heal it until they acknowledge that it wasn't theirs in the first place.*

That's what happened that day in my practice: One acknowledgement that the pain wasn't his allowed the change I hadn't been able to initiate until that point.

When your clients are willing to use the question *Who does this belong to?* they're able to clear any solid energy in their body, and no matter what technique you use — whether you're an MD, a chiropractor, a massage therapist, a reiki practitioner, a physiotherapist — this question is the gateway to allowing you to do your thing and create a greater effect.

How are you feeling about this? It's kind of exciting, right?

I have to say I still get animated about this tool because it plays such a fundamental part in creating change for people that other techniques haven't been able to create.

My friend, with this one awareness you're on the road to having success in your practice that you never thought was possible. More than that – this tool enables you to deepen and expand the communion you're developing with your own body, and allows you to access possibilities beyond the limitations of this reality.

Ready for more? Keep reading.

A New Kind Of Body Language

As we've seen, when we're out of touch with our body and unable to recognize the energetic language it wants to communicate with, and when we're subject to the judgments of others and buying into them ourselves, our bodies have to get our attention in the only way they can: with pain, stiffness and disease — just to communicate whatever awareness we're not listening to.

I'd like to offer you some really practical perspectives on interpreting your body's alternative methods of communicating: a kind of new body language, if you will.

The beauty of what I'm about to share with you is you can use it on yourself and you can bring it into your practice too.

As a reminder, when you experience any kind of physical pain, your first stop is *Who does this belong to?* and if it lightens, it's not yours and you can let it go. What we're looking at here are more questions and tools you can use when it's heavy — in other words, when it does belong to you or when you've bought it as yours.

A great general starting point, if you notice or get a sense of heaviness or intensity when you ask who your pain belongs to, is to follow that up with:

What other question do I need to ask in order to change this?

And also,

What other question do I need to ask in order to get the information to change this?

As always, ask and perceive, and never expect immediate answers.

Now let's get a little more specific in terms of areas of the body where pain commonly presents itself.

Warning: This new kind of body language can be very literal! You might want to kick yourself when you realize how plainly our bodies are speaking to us.

Neck pain

As you're a seeker on a planet full of people wrapped up in judgment and operating from anti-consciousness, you might find yourself noticing how much of a literal pain in the neck this reality is! Yes, a physical pain in the neck really can be the result of a metaphorical one.

Try this:

Ask, *Who or what is the pain in the neck that I'm not acknowledging?* And then add, "Let's destroy and uncreate it. Right and wrong, good and bad, POD & POC, all 9, shorts, boys and beyonds."

Do this a few times because, as I just said, there are opportunities a-plenty in this reality for a metaphorical pain in the neck to present itself in your body. Ask again, *Who or what is the pain in the neck that I'm not acknowledging?* and say the whole clearing statement or just POD & POC it again.

As always, you're not looking for immediate answers — though it's possible you might get them — you're just looking to dissolve that solid energy.

Run the question and the clearing over and over and over and you'll notice the neck pain starts changing.

Lower back pain

Get ready for another really literal message from the body. If you're experiencing back pain, you can ask your body:

What are you hiding behind you?

Yes, again it can be that obvious! This one requires a slightly longer process, because so many of us push our light and our potential for greatness behind us.

> _What are you holding and hiding behind you so dynamically that if you didn't, would make you aware of a level of power, potency, presence and capacity you are not sure you can handle?_ **Right and wrong, good and bad, POD & POC, all 9, shorts, boys and beyonds.**

That is a really wonderful process for allowing you to get access to more of what makes you so amazing and unique, but that you were maybe afraid to really acknowledge. If this idea is feeling light at all to you, please run that process a few more times and really let the light and the space into your world.

Knee pain and foot pain

For knee pain, you can ask:

What needs have you decided you can't handle or can't stand?

For foot pain, ask:

What is it you've decided you can't stand?

Follow up both questions with as many POD & POCs as you require to get the energy to change.

Again, it's all quite obvious, almost too obvious or too easy. In fact, a lot of what I share with the world seems too easy — it puts some people off, which is kind of weird, right?

Is this you?

If so, perhaps you could start by acknowledging that when something is true, it often shows up for us with a sense of ease. Something else to consider is that we have a tendency to dismiss ideas or concepts that are too far beyond what we have previously considered (or decided) can be real or true. In that case, we're rejecting the very reality of beyond-this-reality possibilities that we're here to expand into. If that's the case for you, here's a clearing and a perspective that may help.

What energy, space, consciousness and choice can my body and I be to have total ease perceiving, knowing and receiving all of the ease beyond this reality that my body and I truly be? **Right and wrong, good and bad, POD & POC, all 9, shorts, boys and beyonds.**

And . . . what have I decided are the bounds of reality that I cannot go beyond, cannot experience, and cannot choose that keep me from being the miracles my body and I truly be? **Right and wrong, good and bad, POD & POC, all 9, shorts, boys and beyonds.**

Any ache, pain or aliment on the left side of the body

For anything you experience on the left side of the body, ask:

What are you trying to make right that isn't?

What I find really cool about getting in touch with this new kind of body language is that there's a certain amount of creativity available when you put some of these concepts together.

Say, for example, you or your client has left knee pain. You can put two of the interpretations I've just shared together and ask:

What or whose needs are you trying to make right that are not?

I used this particular one with a client who had a dynamic light-bulb awareness from that one question. "Oh my God!" she said, "My father — he totally needs me and I hate the fact that he needs me and I feel like a bad daughter because he needs me and I don't want to help him out because he's such a mean man…."

The beauty of these questions is that they allow you to start to get the energy of the story your clients are telling themselves, or what they're living with that's creating the physical manifestation of pain.

What are you making of all of this? If nothing else, please know that your body is way more aware than you could ever think.

The further we go with this, the more we realize that people actually know what they're doing when they create their bodies. They know what they're doing when they create their lives, and the symptoms that people come to us with are truly that — they're symptoms. They're aware of something that's going on that they need to change in order to be truly present as them. It's really that simple.

Some Notes on Depression and Anxiety

Have you noticed how those dear souls who experience depression and anxiety are most often labeled the 'sensitive' people of the world? They're shamed for their sensitivity and made to feel that they need to be stronger, more resilient and less emotional. But what if this so-called weakness is actually a source of potency?

I happen to believe that sensitivity is strength. In fact, I believe that any and all of our so-called weaknesses have the capacity to be a source of strength — especially when we become aware of them.

Here's a reality-changing question that can shift your perspective on any feature of your personality that you (or others) have misidentified as a weakness:

What if everything you thought was a wrongness of you is actually a strongness of you?

Take a moment to explore it and see what comes up.

Usually our wrongnesses relate to what we are too much of, or not enough of. For a long time, especially as a kid, I was considered 'too much': too loud, too expressive, too animated, too excited ... the list goes on. It wasn't until I found Access that I was able to recognize this so-called wrongness was actually a natural strength I harbored. In reframing my perception in this way, I was able to open the door to so much more joy, ease, and so much more of ME. I finally exhaled and embraced being 'too much.' Then I took up the space I desired to take up in the world, with zero shame or guilt.

I invite you to take a minute to consider this question for yourself. Let it shine a light on any so-called weaknesses you've bought as true.

Here it is again:

What if everything you thought was a wrongness of you is actually a strongness of you?

Take a moment to imagine what your life could look like if you were to perceive these weaknesses as strengths.

Would you act, think, move, speak and BE different?

Could this new perspective change how you function as a healer?

And could you share this new awareness with your clients?

Reframing the narrative around mental health

This reality is full of those beautiful 'sensitive' souls who are affected and limited by depression and anxiety. You might be one of them (healers often are), or you might not. You will almost certainly have someone in your life — or on your table — who is. So let's take a closer look at what could really be going on for anyone living with depression or anxiety, with a view to deepening our understanding and extending the techniques we use when people come to us for change.

Even though we, as a society, have come a long way in how we view and treat those living with mental health problems, I know we could go further.

Sensitive people don't require a cure and they are no more 'messed up' than other people. Instead, they are so much more AWARE than other people — and in particular they are aware of how messed up so many people in the world feel.

A "normal" person (as if there is such a thing) will perceive the blaring energy of judgment, wrongness, loss of hope and the suffering that so many experience in the world with a volume of two on the stereo of their life. For a 'sensitive' person, their volume dial is turned up to 200.

And, usually, these people are the healer-types (yes, like

you) who feel like no matter what they do, it'll never be
enough to change what they perceive going on in themselves or in the world. They sense all of this without
realizing that they are *perceiving* what is going on in the
world, not truly *being* what they perceive.

Add into the mix that we live in a world where people
are not looked at as individuals, nor are they asked questions to become aware of their unique strengths. Instead,
they're measured according to bell-curves, and mean and
median-distribution standards, and told they are wrong if
they don't fit into the correct box. And these potent, beautiful, 'sensitive' people never fit into the box. They are the
outliers every time.

Alongside all of this, we have to remember that very few
people have the awareness that 98% of the thoughts, feelings, emotions, stress, anxiety, judgment, hopelessness and
depression they experience is something they are perceiving in the world around them.

Take all of this together and it's easy to see this reality has
created a dynamic incongruence and a sense of futility in
the world of anyone battling depression or anxiety.... An
incongruence that you are now better prepared to contribute to changing than ever before.

How does it get any better than that?

First: Two things you can do today if you feel depressed or anxious yourself

In a moment I'm going to take you through some tools for working with people in your practice who are living with depression or anxiety, but before we get to that I just want to offer two suggestions for you, dear reader, if you're battling with any of these conditions yourself. Please know you are not alone and there are the people and the tools here to help you. I have walked this path myself and speak to you with care from a place of experience.

First and foremost, I recommend you look into taking an Access Consciousness Bars Class (you can find details of classes near you on our website, listed toward the back of this book). An Access Bars session is a hands-on energy modality that has a phenomenal capacity to get you to a place where you let go of all your limiting beliefs, thoughts and ideas. A Bars class was my gateway into Access and I highly recommend it.

Secondly, I urge you to use *Who Does This Belong To?* for three days for all the thoughts, feelings and emotions you experience. I've mentioned this before but it's worth mentioning again because, seriously, it worked so well for me. Head back to Chapter 4 to recap on how to introduce it, or re-read the section earlier in this chapter, 'Tapping further into your body as a psychic receiver' which explores it in more depth.

This one question, *Who does this belong to?*, really is the key to the process of change. It's something that will get you out of the big scary hole that depression feels like, and it's the beginning of accessing the potency and the power within you to know you have the capacity to change.

Four key ways to work with a client who is depressed or anxious

1. Be aware of how you perceive them before anything else. As a body whisperer one of your gifts is your capacity to recognize the strength of the person underneath the condition, and in this case it's essential for you to recognize the person underneath what often manifests as depression.

2. Introduce the idea to your client that their 'sensitivity' is a power, not a weakness.

3. Make them aware of the concept behind *Who Does This Belong To?* (that 98% of the thoughts, feelings and so on are NOT theirs, and are in fact what they are perceiving). Really encourage them to use the tool. We have a free *Who Does This Belong To?* mobile app. Just search "Access Consciousness Who Does This Belong To?"

4. This point should really be first. The most powerful

way you can initiate change for someone dealing with depression or anxiety is by *being you with them, with no judgment.*

You can do that easily and naturally.

I know it.

Is it time for YOU to know it?

See? You really are more prepared than you thought.

Just by BEING YOU.

Taking a Client From Tired To Limitless

Depending on your training and the type of work that you do on people's bodies, you may have a go-to set of supplements and processes for certain conditions. For example, some practitioners believe that if a client is presenting with anger issues, there's something going on with the liver, so they'll work on processing the liver for emotions as a means to assist with that. In a similar way, some practitioners offer adrenal supplements to those clients who have lethargy and low energy.

While there's nothing wrong with either of those choices, what if you just asked this question:

Body, what is it that you require to have the energy you desire?

The beautiful thing about this is that you can just ask the body, you don't need to verbally ask the client. Silently ask the question and then run the clearing:

> *Body, what is it that you require to have the energy you desire? Everything that doesn't allow it, will you destroy and uncreate it please?* **Right and wrong, good and bad, POD & POC, all 9, shorts, boys and beyonds.**

When you're present with a person and their body, you'll recognize that their body will communicate different things than the person themselves — you just have to be willing to ask it.

Why is tiredness so prevalent in our society?

It's actually really simple: All of the judgments, decisions, conclusions and computations that we make on a daily basis literally work to clog us up, stopping our energy from doing that beautiful free-flow that it naturally desires to do. The result: tiredness, lethargy and low, low energy.

Try this: Run this clearing with all the clients you have who are stopping themselves from accessing limitless energy:

> *All the decisions, the judgments, the conclusions and computations that you have, or that you are buying from others as yours, will you destroy and uncreate it please?* ***Right and wrong, good and bad, POD & POC, all 9, shorts, boys and beyonds.***

Along with the huge amounts of judgment, the other big creator of low energy stems from the fact so many people want to get out of their life the way it is now.

Try this: Ask a client who's experiencing low energy this question: "How's your life going?" They might be a little taken aback if they're not expecting an alternative practitioner to talk to them about something other than their main complaint, but usually (as we looked at in Chapter 8: Congruency) an open question like this can work to open a door to the real issue and the real reason they're seeing you.

What you might get is an answer like, "I'm so tired. I've got four kids to take care of and a busy husband, and I'm just really stressed. I don't know how I'm going to make the money last to the end of the month, and the bills are due, and my husband just won't talk about it. I have zero energy."

This is good, and it can get better.

Let me give you a question that you can ask this client, and all of your clients, to start to unlock awarenesses and change their tiredness. Are you ready? It's so simple you're going to (at best) roll your eyes or (at worst) throw the book across the room.

Here it is:

What (or who) are you tired of?

Really.

Now, when you first bring this question into a session, you might need to ask it a couple of times, but what you might find is that the lady with the four kids and the husband who won't communicate might say something like this after a moment or two, "You know what? I'm tired of cleaning up everyone else's mess. Mostly, I'm tired of being the responsible one."

And bingo: There's something you can work on with her.

Can I just ask you something, dear reader?

How are your energy levels? Are you often tired?

Let's face it, most of us don't always have the energy we'd like to have and the energy we're entitled to have. Would you like to use this next question on yourself?

Here it is:

What (or who) are you tired of that you don't want to acknowledge?

Now just get a sense of what comes up with that. Remember, you don't need definite answers. Ever. You just need to be open enough to ask the question.

What are you tired of that you don't want to acknowledge?

Now run it with the clearing statement:

What are you tired of that you don't want to acknowledge? Everything that is, will you destroy and uncreate it please? **Right and wrong, good and bad, POD & POC, all 9, shorts, boys and beyonds.**

When I ran this question on the video series which this book is based on, I ran it five times because I really wanted the participants to get light on this, and start to get a change from it — because how are we going to try to bring lightness to other people when we don't have lightness ourselves?

Make sense? I thought it would.

One more time:

What are you tired of that you don't want to acknowledge? Everything that is, will you destroy and uncreate it please? **Right and wrong, good and bad, POD & POC, all 9, shorts, boys and beyonds.**

Do you notice you're feeling a little more alive? I know I do whenever I use this tool. Its impact never diminishes.

Notice how each time you ask yourself that question and run the clearing, it takes a little piece of your tiredness away, and a little more, and a little more. After three, four or five times you might just find you're not actually tired anymore.

<u>Realize that most people walking around on the planet are tired of everything _all of the time._</u> If you can initiate a change in this area, you'll have people flocking to your practice.

Simply ask, _What, or who, are you tired of? Will you destroy and uncreate it?_ And then run the clearing statement — again, you can do this under your breath or say it out loud — it's your call. Whatever suits you and whatever they're willing to receive.

Remember that you're not looking for your clients to verbally answer this, or any, question. The clearing statement will do its miraculous thing by going back to the point wherever they created the problem in the first place — and that's something they might not even remember.

What are you tired of that you're not acknowledging is one of the most dynamic tools you can offer to change the lack of energy that people have. It's the quickest way to undo all of the judgment, conclusion, decision and computation which just drags us down.

I'd like to take a second to say that this question, and all of the questions I suggest to you in this book, can be seen as a starting point. They're included because I find them effective and I've had results with them, but as you try these questions out you'll naturally come up with others that suit you and your practice. Experiment and explore what works for you. And remember that a question is always about opening a way to a different possibility.

Your clients don't know there's a different possibility — until they meet you. Your questions will create possibilities that they didn't know could exist. And you'll be one of the greatest gifts in their life.

It's About The Person On The Table

If you're a body whisperer who is practicing from consciousness, so that you're in allowance of everything and anything your client presents to you, and you're out of judgment and you're in the question, then please believe this: Any blocks that come up in a session, any weird feelings, any sense of unease or powerlessness that you experience — it's coming from the person on the table or in the chair: your client — and not from you.

Even when what comes up really, *really* feels like it's yours, it's really, *really* not.

Knowing this, and recognizing it, is such a liberating thing! What you're perceiving is part of your skill, and part of your gift as a body whisperer.

Let's look at an example. Say you're halfway through a session and you suddenly feel really insecure about what you're doing. Just a moment ago you were in full flow, doing what you do, and then — a cloud descends, and you suddenly think: *I can't do this. I'm not powerful enough.*

This feeling will feel like it's coming from you, and it might even be familiar, personalized even — to the extent that you associate it with a specific time in your past when you experienced powerlessness or insecurity.

This feels just like when my dad left my mom.

This feels exactly how it did when my high school teacher said I'd never amount to anything.

As convincing as it might seem, please know that if you're practicing from presence and allowance — where there is no judgment, no alignment or agreement, no resistance and reaction — that insecure and powerless feeling is something your talented and gifted sponge-like body is picking up from the person on the table.

Do you see how amazing and useful this is? You've perceived what they're going through and now you get to work on it. You were led to exactly where your client is stuck — and it's likely that nobody else in the universe has been to this place with them before you. And, if they have, they most likely backed off and shut down because they took it on as their own.

Any time you're working on someone and you suddenly feel something like insecurity, powerlessness or — my particular favorite (not!) — you feel like you're in a white room with white walls and no windows and no doors and no way in and no way out … just play with this idea:

What if that's theirs? What if that's what my client is experiencing?

This is you energetically getting the awareness of what is going on in their world. *They* are feeling insecure, or powerless, or blank. This is the way their body and the universe is working to give you that energy so you can work with them to create something far, far greater than what they can access and create on their own.

That's why they're there with you: to try to get beyond the wall that they don't know how to get beyond.

Think of it this way: We're all part of the universe. Our molecules are communicating with each other all the time. Their world is interacting with yours and when you recognize this is what's happening, and when you acknowledge that you're not separate from them, or the universe, you understand that you're picking up on the energy of what they require. No more taking it on as your own!

It was just so freeing when I finally got this. Is it creating a little tingle of freedom for you too? I'm sure it can't be that easy … can it?

This is the wonder of how it feels when a healing session is really working — for both you and your client. Every session has its own route or path, and as you venture down it you unlock layers and layers to uncover what it is your client requires. It's incredible when this happens — and it's also your brilliant capacities that enable it to happen.

Be aware that what your client requires might not be something they can actually talk about. In fact, it's likely that they don't even know it's there. In recognizing what you picked up is about them, you remain present and alongside them, and from there you can facilitate a change.

The danger comes when we buy the notion that it's our insecurity that has thrown us off course, and we think we're failing somehow.

Sound familiar? Run this:

> *Everywhere you've been making you wrong, because you don't believe that you're actually a good enough healer because let's face it, we judge the crap out of ourselves more than anybody else ever would or could, will you destroy and uncreate that, and all of the judgments, all of the inventions, all of the lies that you bought, all the projections, all the expectations, all the separations and all the rejections of you and your capacities that you've done with that, will you destroy and uncreate it please?* **Right and wrong, good and bad, POD & POC, all 9, shorts, boys and beyonds.**

When we stop the energy

If you're midway through a session and you suddenly buy the idea that you're not enough, or if you doubt your capacity to initiate change, you effectively stop the session. You stop the energy, and you stop the miraculous change that you were in the process of facilitating.

Please. Read that paragraph again.

It might feel like a wall has been thrown up, or it might suddenly feel like you're wading through treacle (that's British for the stuff that lives in a cesspool, by the way). The quickest way to deal with this is to ask yourself:

Is this my stuck or theirs?

Then, *Am I having the exact energy of where they're stuck? Or am I having AWARENESS of the exact energy of where they're stuck?*

Suddenly there's a shift from:

Oh God, I'm stuck!

to

Oh — this is where THEY'RE stuck! Awesome.

Now you get to facilitate them to go beyond that place —
and the energy flows again. (For some of you, this one
awareness, if you use it, may be worth the price of this book!)

Feeling versus awareness

Notice the difference between these two statements:

> *I feel powerless.*

And

> *I'm aware of a sense of powerlessness.*

The first one is personal, because you're taking the powerlessness on and attributing it to you. You *feel* contracted
and small.

Right now, just take a moment to imagine the energy of
powerlessness and insecurity. Do you notice how small and
contracted your world becomes?

The second statement, *I'm aware of a sense of powerlessness,* is
more objective; there's a step back, a bit of distance. You're
aware of powerlessness. You take a side-step that allows
you to do your job.

From that point you stand back and you get bigger, and

you can look at what has come into your awareness, and ask, *What can I do and what can I be to change this for them?*

I won't tell you how you should do this, but I can share with you how I do it and, as ever, you're welcome to try it.

In Practice: Being the energy I'm perceiving

Here's what works for me. In essence, *I be* what I'm perceiving. I *be* something that encompasses this universe of whatever my client is going through. So, if they've thrown up a wall — I be the wall.

Let me go into this in a little more detail by setting the scene.

I'm midway through a session with a client, the energy is moving and we're exploring these universes and possibilities and things are expanding and changing and moving and expanding and I'm thinking how awesome this is and then —

— imagine a rug being pulled from under me, or a pin popping a balloon, or a brick wall being thrown up right in front of me, practically touching my nose … and the energy just … stops.

Years ago, before I had the awareness that everything is about the person on the table, I would straight away go into thoughts like this: *Oh my God, what am I doing wrong? What am I being wrong? What have I stopped here? What did I miss? What didn't I do?*

Basically, I'd personalize what I was perceiving and blame myself. In truth, this happened quite a few times before I understood it to the extent that I can now share it with you. I'm so glad to be able to share it — hopefully you won't take as long to have your penny-drop moment.

My penny-drop moment came when I spoke to Gary about it. I explained how there was this one particular client who I was working on, and how midway through my sessions with him this wall would get thrown up and I'd get stuck and not know what to do, and once the wall was up, I couldn't figure out where to go and how to get past it.

And Gary said, "So, is it your wall or his?"

And I said, "F**k!"

Until that moment I assumed it was mine. It sure felt like mine. Tricky, sneaky, crafty wall! It was the client's all along. Of course it was — because when I acknowledged it, I knew I was practicing from presence, out of judgment, and in allowance.

Have you ever had one of those moments where you just

want to scream and explode the universe because your realization is so big yet so obvious that you think you should have been able to figure it out yourself? But you didn't — until somebody asked you the question? It was very much like that.

By the way — isn't it amazing how often it goes that way — how often a question unlocks the exact awareness you need? I think so.

I was so grateful for that new awareness — *it belongs to the person on the table* — and with that awareness and acknowledgement I was in a place to facilitate change for this client. Here's how it played out.

At my very next session with this guy and his wall, I began with my usual question to get him congruent. "If you could have anything out of this session, what would it be?" and he said, "I just want to be happy and free and I want to feel like I'm connected to things."

The energy was congruent with the ask, so I thought — great, let's do this. Then, at the usual spot in our sessions, the wall came up. This time, instead of running away and going into, "Oh God, what's wrong with me?" and effectively stopping the energy of what we were creating, I became the energy of the wall.

How? I lowered all of my barriers and I got right up to that wall, and energetically I said: "Hi."

I stood in front of the wall and I became the 10,000 lb. gorilla in the room.

The wall, of course, wasn't going to crumble and dissolve right away. It was a big wall, stubborn and persistent. The wall and I had a bit of to-and-fro that went something like:

The Wall: I am a big wall and you must go away!

Me: Cool. Awesome. You're an awesome wall. Hi.

The Wall: No, you don't understand! I'm a big bad wall and if you go any further, I'm going to kill you.

Me: Awesome. I'm ready. Hi.

The Wall: No, you're terrible! You're small. You should not be here. Go back.

Me: Awesome. Hi.

The wall tried every trick it knew to keep me away — which, I soon realized — was exactly what the person was doing: trying to keep themselves out of their own life and keep other people away and out of their life.

I stayed standing despite everything the wall threw at me, responding mainly with a "Hi!" until ... wait for it ... the wall just ... dissolved.

And then ... there was a palpable sense of the energy in this client's world changing. Not just changing, but exploding, igniting, accelerating.

Remember his ask at the start of the session? "I just want to be happy and free and I want to feel like I'm connected to things." When the wall came down this person energetically leapt out from his own small and constricted world — the one he'd asked me to get him out of — and his joy increased, his sense of connection increased and he was *free*. *It was sooo beautiful to perceive!*

Whether he knew it cognitively or not, he'd constructed the wall. It was the thing keeping him from being that connection that he asked for.

By just being with the wall, lowering my barriers and saying, "Hi," to every insult, to every profanity, to everything that wall had in its arsenal to throw at me, it dissolved, and then came a profound sense of peace in this guy's world, and he took this really deep breath. It was intense, in a brilliant way. I put my hands on his body again and it was like my hand melted into his world.

Whenever you experience those feelings of insecurity, of doubt, of fear, of constriction during a session, you now have the tools to get past them. And yes, it's no more complicated than that. Remember, this is transformation (healing if you prefer) from *BEING*.

If I may recap ...

You're practicing from allowance, where everything is just an interesting point of view. You're in the question, where chaos flows.

Your client's biggest insecurity or fear comes up, and you know that no matter how much it feels like *your* biggest insecurity or fear — it's not.

As you recognize it's theirs you stay present, you lower your own barriers even more, and you stay there, by their side, and you be the energy of what you're perceiving — or you practice whatever modality works for you. Being the energy works for me.

In essence, you are being the energy with and for them that they can't yet be with and for themselves.

You can also use the following questions:

What question can I ask to assist them in changing this?

What question can I be that will assist them in changing this?

What question can I ask and what question can I be that will assist them in changing this?

Your gift is to be something they haven't ever been able to be for themselves, but that the two of you together are in a unique position to take on.

Please recognize that the people who come to you are coming to you because there's something you, and you alone, can facilitate for them. They're coming to you for the change that you can gift. They're coming to you because there's a unique interaction between you and them. And there's a unique facilitation that you can do that nobody else on the planet can, including me. They're coming to you because you are the one who can contribute to them.

How does it get any more beautiful and awesome than that?

When You're Stuck

Whether you've been practicing for a day or a decade, there comes a time on your body whispering path when you get the sense that you're just not creating the change you know you can. Maybe your work starts to feel like a chore, or you notice you're very lackluster about it, or you find yourself frustrated with your clients because of what they're choosing or not choosing. Whichever way you look at it — it's just not lighting your fire anymore.

Believe me, I've been there, and I'm here to tell you: It's okay. You can *so* relight that fire. It's usually really easy — when you ask the right questions. I have five umbrella questions here for you, some with other questions under them, all of which have the capacity to strike the match to get that fire going again.

Let's look at each big question in turn.

1. Are you resisting your capacities?

It might sound like an odd question to ask at this point in the book, but for anyone who's not fully working in their capacity as a healer I'd start by looking at whether there's any resistance occurring. In particular I'd ask: *Could you be resisting your capacities, your talent and your gift in some way?*

For a lot of body whisperers, this isn't their first rodeo — they've been body whispering in previous lives and incarnations, whether they were aware that's what they were doing back then or not.

Is it possible that you had an experience in a previous life-time in which your naturally empathic nature led you to take on so much pain and suffering that you decided it was too painful to be a healer, too painful to have that much power, or too painful to have that much awareness?

Is it possible that you decided *I'm never going to do this again?*

If that's feeling light at all, first, please recognize that was then, this is now. You have so much more awareness available to you now.

> <u>Whatever was done to make you decide you didn't</u> <u>want to be a healer, didn't want to be empathic, didn't</u> <u>want to have that much power, didn't want to have</u> <u>that much awareness, will you now destroy and uncre-</u> <u>ate it please?</u> ***Right and wrong, good and bad, POD*** ***& POC, all 9, shorts, boys and beyonds.***

No matter what you've gone through in any lifetime, even if you were walking through places where a nuclear bomb had exploded, and your healing of others took so much from you that your body died painfully and it led you to decide, *I never want to do this again,* please don't let that be the reason you close down the ability and the gift you naturally have as a being in this lifetime.

How can you turn this around? Instead of thinking, *I don't want to do this, I don't want to feel this, I don't want to be this aware,* what if instead you would allow yourself to say:

You know what? Yes, I had some experiences in the past that may have made me want to stop this, but in this lifetime I'm going to do it, I'm going to be it. I'm going to claim and own my healing capacities so that I know how to use them so my body doesn't have to hurt. So I don't have to feel like I'm alone in this world, and so I can actually do what I came here to do.

> *Everything that doesn't allow that, in other words —*
> *everything that doesn't allow you to claim and own*
> *your healing capacities and the brilliance of that, every-*
> *where you've decided to give that up as though that*
> *would somehow free you from this thing that you do*
> *of taking on everybody else's pain and suffering, and*
> *everywhere you've decided this is too much, it's too*
> *much awareness, it's too much power, I don't want to*
> *do it — will you please now destroy and uncreate it?*
> ***Right and wrong, good and bad, POD & POC, all***
> ***9, shorts, boys and beyonds.***

The very reason why you got into healing in the first place, why you picked up this book, why you're this far into it — is to reconnect with the magnificence of being able to gift other people a different possibility in their lives, and the magnificence of being able to change where people are in pain and help them get out of pain.

And … beyond that, perhaps … to actually contribute to creating a world of possibilities … and magic … and miracles … and joy….

Can you acknowledge that? You are so brilliant, and such a light. I thank you for being here. On this beautiful planet. Right now.

2. Are you in the question?

Whenever you're running a session and you suddenly get stuck, and you know you're not creating the change you know you can — head for the question. Always. Just quickly check in with yourself — *Am I healing from the question? Or am I simply looking for answers?* Remember, answers, cures, conclusions — all of these have a very solid energy where change is unlikely.

Questions on the other hand offer space, expansiveness and possibility. From there you get to perceive those areas of solidity in the bodies you're working on.

Here are some question suggestions for those times when you feel stuck:

> *What question can I ask here to get the awareness so I can facilitate this person?*

What question am I not asking that if I asked it would allow me to assist this person?

What else is possible?

What is possible beyond-this-reality that I think is not possible, that if I simply allowed the possibility would actualize a different, greater reality?

How does it get any better than this?

What am I aware of, and what am I capable of, that I have not been choosing and acknowledging that would allow this to change?

Anytime that you feel confounded, like someone grabbed all your power and your gift just left you and you can't remember the questions I just suggested and it's all feeling pretty big and scary — it's okay. I have four simple questions for you which are freakin' fantastic. I highly recommend you have these four questions in your arsenal ready to use at all times — for when you're working on people, and for when you're navigating your way through life and you're just not sure how to move forward or through a tricky situation.

Here they are:

What is this really?

What do I do with it?

Can I change it?

And if so, how do I change it?

What these four beautiful questions do is keep you well away from the door marked YOU ARE WRONG. I know way too many healers who have a tendency to run through that door when they're not creating the change they know they can — personally or professionally.

Please, when this happens, go to the question instead of going to the wrongness of you, and I assure you that you have a much better shot of going beyond that stuck place. And remember ... there's a really, really good chance that what you're picking up on is from the client, and it's the exact thing they require your assistance with.

Oh, and an FYI, *What am I doing wrong?* is not a question! It's a judgment disguised as a question.

Cunning, huh?! Until you see it, then it's really obvious.

Here are those four beautifully adaptable questions once more:

What is this really?

What do I do with it?

Can I change it?

And if so, how do I change it?

When you use them, notice the space they bring. Any 'problem' gets so spacious and happy you can almost hear angels laughing and flapping their wings in your general direction.

Wouldn't it be awesome if, while you're doing a session, you had this really easy way of going beyond it, provided by four big little questions?

Oh, wait — now you do!

3. Are you vested in the outcome?

This is a biggie. If you choose to work on the bodies of people you care about (and that might just be everyone, caring being that you are) being vested in the outcome is a trap you may easily fall into without even realizing it.

When you're vested in the outcome, you're harboring a really strong want or need for your client to change. For whatever reason, you're holding on with a very firm vice-like grip, with clenched muscles and clenched teeth, willing your client to choose what you think they should choose. Basically, you're up to your neck in judgments and points of view, and you're communicating this: "You should change, you should change, you should change."

Even though what you're doing comes from a place of caring, what your client is receiving from you is judgment. Solid, immovable judgment. They'll be getting a sense of guilt and wrongness, and is change likely to happen from that solid place? I think you know the answer to that.

Here's your clearing for those situations when you're really vested in the outcome. Please, please, please use it!

> *Everything I'm doing to be vested in the outcome, everything I have aligned and agreed with, everything I've resisted and reacted to that makes me not be in allowance of them changing or not changing, let's destroy and uncreate it please?* **Right and wrong, good and bad, POD & POC, all 9, shorts, boys and beyonds.**

What if, when you're working on someone you care about, you were to cultivate a sense of: "Hi, I'm here. You can change or not, that's your choice."

Do you get what a totally different space of being that is? It's free of judgment, it's true allowance. That's the space that allows people to change because — please realize — a lot of the things people will come to you for are related to issues they've been judged for their whole lives — and they've probably been judging themselves about these things for a very long time, too. So is it any surprise that the energy of not being "enough" to change it, or their judgment of not changing it yet, or their belief that it will never change, will rear its interestingly ugly head?

Be the space of allowance and see how much more you can do, be and gift. *And enjoy.*

4. Are you bored?

If you've been practicing for a while, and you're getting good results, but then ... you realize you're plateauing somewhat, and the very thought of working on people is making you go, 'Meh,' then I'm willing to bet it's because you're functioning from: *I have people who have back pain. I do this. I have people who have cancer. I do this. I have people who have musculoskeletal problems, and I do this.*

It's very ordered. Very A + B = C. Not very chaotic, not very conscious, and not at all creative. Not to mention: not at all YOU!

When things plateau, it's usually because you're functioning from answers and conclusions and order, so I would always suggest a good dose of chaos in these situations. How? Be more in the question to see what else is possible.

Try this:

> *What question can you be and ask that you haven't been choosing to be and ask, that if you chose to be it and ask it, would lighten up everything in your practice?* ***Everything that doesn't allow it, right and wrong, good and bad, POD & POC, all 9, shorts, boys and beyonds.***

5. Are you resenting work?

Now this next page or so might be really terrifying or exciting for you, depending on your point of view around money and receiving money as a healer. Luckily I have a whole chapter dedicated to just that and it's coming right up. Maybe you've already peeked at it? I wouldn't blame you — it's a BIG area for body whisperers!

For now, I just want to put it to you that, when you start to resent doing sessions, when you don't want to go to your practice anymore, when you don't want to work on people, when it's not fun for you anymore, 99% of the time it's because you're not charging enough.

I've been through it myself and I had no idea it was connected to money. I'm going to explore it with you in depth in the next chapter, but for now, here's a question you can ask if, or when, you get the sense that your work isn't fun and you're not creating the change you know you're capable of:

> *How much would I have to charge for this to be*
> *fun again?*

Get the energy of that and bravely step into Chapter 12, my friend.

CHAPTER
12

Knowing Your Value As A Healer—Do You Deserve To Get Paid?

If there's one question guaranteed to induce a ton of issues, sticking points and sweaty palms for body whisperers across the globe, it's this one:

Is it okay to get paid for doing this?

Sound familiar? And what about this one: *Is it okay to get paid **well** for doing this?*

Be honest, do you think that you, as a healer, should be paid really well? How about six-figures well? How about more than that?

If you're feeling confused, scared, or resisting or reacting in any way with this, I assure you: You are not alone, and I'm so happy to be able to share this chapter with you because, believe me, I've been there too.

Back when I first found Access I had so many misgivings around getting paid for the work I did on people, and this was intensified by, and intermingled with, a whole heap of issues I had around money and receiving in general.

In fact, as my good and sage friend Gary said to me many years ago, "Dain, you don't have money issues. Your issues are around what you're willing to receive."

Talk about a light-bulb moment! And, incidentally, that's just the first of many I'll share with you in this chapter. Gary was right, of course, I had such an issue with receiving in general — not just with money. This is often the case; you think you have a money issue and actually what's holding you back is rooted in receiving of all kinds.

It took letting go of my limiting beliefs and embracing some new awarenesses — all of which I'm about to share with you — to get to the place where I now have total ease — and joy (gasp) — around charging for the work I do.

By the way, did you feel a twinge of recognition when I said I had issues with receiving? Then it may be true for you too. Run this:

What have you decided receiving is, that it isn't? Everything that is, times a godzillion, will you destroy and uncreate it, please? **Right and wrong, good and bad, POD & POC, all 9, shorts, boys and beyonds.**

And....

What have you decided receiving isn't, that it is? Everything that is, times a godzillion, will you destroy and uncreate it, please? **Right and wrong, good and bad, POD & POC, all 9, shorts, boys and beyonds.**

I'm hopeful that in sharing what kept me stuck and limited around money I can now, in turn, bring these into your awareness too, because, dear healer: You absolutely deserve to be paid, and paid well, for the change you facilitate.

We're about to lift the lid on the three most common limiting beliefs for healers and explore some new awarenesses around money that can initiate a phenomenal shift in perspective. If this speaks to you, expect to be taken to a place where you finally see that you deserve to be paid well for what you do, *and* that what you earn reflects the gift that you are and the change you can create, *and* it enables you to access your actual capacities and potential as a healer.

Let's start with those limiting beliefs.

Limiting point of view #1: You should work for free

*... and if you do charge people, you should just charge a
tiny amount. And don't ever increase your rates. Actually, you know what — just work for free.*

There's a dominant point of view that a lot of people across
the planet hold and it goes like this:

If you're doing something good for people, you should do
it for free.

There's this sense that, especially when you're gifted with
something, you have a duty to share that gift and you
should share it with zero financial reward for you. After
all, you're a healer so you shouldn't be concerned with
all that material stuff, should you? And if you are, you're
greedy, and you're taking advantage of people, when you
really ought to be totally selfless and spiritual.

Talk about a limiting point of view! Not to mention
one overflowing with judgment and therefore very, very
destructive.

The truth is we all have bills to pay and we all need to eat, and
as conscious as we may be, that alone isn't going to sustain
us in this reality. To continue to work as a healer, a changer,
a body whisperer, payment is what makes it sustainable.

Please, don't take this limiting view on as your own, don't buy into it or let it fuel any of the misgivings you might have about setting your rates as a practicing healer. Don't deprive the world of your gift, of the unique invitation you are.

Ready to let it go? Note: Some of you might want to run this several times:

> _Everywhere that you bought the idea that you should work for free or very little, will you destroy and uncreate it please?_ **Right and wrong, good and bad, POD & POC, all 9, shorts, boys and beyonds.**

And….

> _Everywhere that you bought the idea that because you're doing "spiritual" or "healing" work that you owe it to people for free, will you destroy and uncreate it please?_ **Right and wrong, good and bad, POD & POC, all 9, shorts, boys and beyonds.**

Limiting point of view #2: Money is the root of all evil

Before we get into this one, let's get it factually correct: Money as the root of evil is one of the most misquoted and misunderstood lines from the Bible. The actual quote is *The love of money is the root of all evil*, which is a different thing all together. Think about it: Money itself has no inherent badness about it. The five or ten or fifty dollar bill in your wallet has no inherent badness (or goodness) about it.

Things only get problematic when your love of money *is greater than* your love of creation, and when you value money over all else, in particular the contribution and gift you can be to others.

When you look at it this way it's pretty straightforward: You can enjoy and appreciate money without it being the most valuable product in your life. You can be willing to have it without it running — *or ruining* — your life.

Limiting point of view #3:
Making money is hard / It's not okay to have fun and make money / I don't deserve to have a lot of money anyway

(Basically any point of view about money you picked up from your parents.)

(And anyone else in your life.)

Remember how we soak up all the beliefs, judgments and points of view of everyone around us?

Here's a question:

> *Is it possible you've been buying someone else's financial reality as yours when it isn't actually yours?*
>
> *And whose reality might that be?*

It makes sense that a lot of us have probably taken on the financial reality of our parents or whoever raised us. Take a moment to think about what the attitude and atmosphere was around money when you were a kid.

Was money scarce, or was it abundant? If it was scarce, chances are there was a lot of stress and worry attached to money, and understandably so.

The thing is, even in households where money doesn't appear to be an issue, there can still be underlying anxieties around it. Often the wealthiest people are the most reluctant to spend and enjoy their wealth, because their money mindset is one of scarcity, even when their reality shows lots of money. If you have issues with receiving, it's not as simple as 'you were raised rich or you were raised poor' — often it goes a lot deeper than that.

The wonderful thing is you now have the choice to let go of any financial realities which don't belong to you. Whatever money mindset you've picked up along the course of your life, you can now choose to free yourself of it, and this will free you up in so many ways to enjoy receiving money for the amazing work you do.

> *Whose financial reality are you buying as real and true for you that isn't? Everything that is, times a godzillion, will you destroy and uncreate it please?* **Right and wrong, good and bad, POD & POC, all 9, shorts, boys and beyonds.**

Something else to consider is that as a healer you may have picked up on the financial realities of other people who do similar work to you. If you've encountered other healers on your way to here who either did it for free or believed you should work for very little, could you have taken their point of view as your reality?

Run the clearing again:

> *Whose financial reality are you buying as real and*
> *true for you that isn't? Everything that is, times a*
> *godzillion, will you destroy and uncreate it please?*
> **Right and wrong, good and bad, POD & POC, all**
> **9, shorts, boys and beyonds.**

Now, those are just three of the common limiting beliefs that healers often have to contend with whether they're new to practicing or whether they've been doing it for years. If you can let go of those, or at least see them for what they are: very limiting, probably not yours, and potentially very destructive, then your reality around money and earning as a healer can start to change beyond your wildest imaginings.

Ready for some awarenesses?

New awareness #1:
You can be conscious *and* desire (and have) money

Yes, these two things can absolutely go together! I'm sure that what brought you to this line of work was a desire to contribute to people, gift to people, and create a change in the world. With that in mind, I'd be surprised if money is the main driver or influence in why you're a healer, or why you're considering taking the step to practicing as a healer.

Yes, there's a 'however' on the way…. Here's the thing: Just because you don't want to make money your number one focus, it doesn't mean you shouldn't have or desire the money that will allow you to create a fulfilling life for you and the people that you care about.

If this is feeling light for you, I invite you to give yourself permission to actually have money, and to embrace the idea of making money as a healer, and to be at ease with desiring money.

It doesn't make you greedy or bad in any way. While it's true that there's a lot of greed in the world, and plenty of money-focused people in power — just because that's how they 'do' having money, doesn't mean that you do it that way, or from that place.

Again: There is nothing inherently bad about money. You can be conscious *and* desire money.

> *All the lies you bought about people with money and how bad they are and how terrible and you never wanted to be one – all of that, will you destroy and uncreate it please?* **Right and wrong, good and bad, POD & POC, all 9, shorts, boys and beyonds.**

By the way, I bought into the lie that I couldn't be conscious and wealthy too, which is why I couldn't afford rent before I started using these Access Consciousness tools.

New awareness #2:
There's a connection between how much you charge and the amount of change you can create — *and* the amount of change that people will allow

This is such a big one. In my early days of being in Access, I was still a practicing chiropractor and I charged $25 a session. During a conversation with Gary, he asked what kind of results I was creating for that fee, and I told him how on the one hand some people were getting amazing results, but how on the whole I had this sense that what I was creating wasn't close to what I knew was possible.

Gary, with his ability to get to the crux of an issue said, "It's because you're not charging enough."

I have to admit I was confused; I'd expected him to impart advice about a technique or maybe offer up a tool, so I asked what he meant, and he said, "How much change are people willing to receive when they pay you $25?"

I still wasn't clear on where he was going, so he put it a little plainer for me. "Dain, $25 is about two movie tickets. By paying you $25, that's the amount of change your clients are willing to have."

Ah — okay — now I was starting to get it! If I charged roughly the same amount as the price of a movie ticket, people would allow the amount of change that they would get out of a movie. And how much change do people get out of movies? Not much, and it's not very long-lasting.

This was my first step toward understanding more about valuing myself. In fact, it created a massive shift in my awareness, because it allowed me to see that getting paid was directly related to the change I was able to create in people's lives — and more than anything else, I wanted to work with people to create healing and change in their lives.

New awareness #3:
The purpose of having money is to change people's lives for the greater

This perspective was offered to me, again, by the astute and awareness-initiating Gary, when he asked me, "Can you change the world more with money or without money?"

It seemed like a no-brainer: "With money, of course," I replied.

"That's right," he said, "and the purpose of money is to change people's realities for the greater."

This was (another!) one of those wow-moments for me! It was the first time anybody had given me the perspective that money could do good, great and incredible things. It was so exciting and motivating. From that point forward my financial situation started to change.

> *Everything you've done to make it wrong to charge for your services, and everywhere you have that weird catch in your throat when you go to tell people how much you charge, and you feel like of course you must be charging too much, will you destroy and uncreate it please?* ***Right and wrong, good and bad, POD & POC, all 9, shorts, boys and beyonds.***

I really hope that these new awarenesses will bring you a sense of ease around the whole issue of money, because I know how much it can hold your gift back.

Next, let's look at what to consider when you set your rates.

In practice: Setting your rates

I have two really awesome questions you can ask yourself to get tuned in with what your rates should be. They're woven into this next story, where I'll show you how I personally used these questions to finally get over my issues with receiving.

Back in my early days of doing Access and developing the energy work that I do, Gary came to see me for a session. At the start, he suggested that I ask his body what it required. This was the first time I'd come across the concept of asking the body what it wants — interesting as it's now so central to how I practice!

In truth, back then I had no idea what Gary meant. After a little hesitation I tried it: I asked his body what it required, I tapped into the energy of it, and I began creating change in Gary's body unlike anything either of us had ever experienced before. What transpired in that session was the genesis, the beginning, of the ESB (Energetic Synthesis of Being) modality that I now practice and teach worldwide.

This experience was like a door opening to a new world of possibilities for me as a healer, so when Gary invited me to do ESB sessions at the next advanced Access class I was so excited. Then came the big question: "So Dain, how much are you going to charge?"

Ah, hello money and receiving issues! I had no idea what to say so I decided to seek the advice of an experienced Access facilitator who asked me a question which was so useful and powerful and which I am so happy to be sharing with you. She said:

> *What would be so exciting to charge that you feel almost scared to ask for it, but if you got it would make you so happy?*

Seriously, read that again, underline it, write it in your notebook, your phone memos — because it is such a gift of a question.

I took a second to think about it before giving her my answer. And in what genuinely felt like a reach-for-the-stars moment for me I said, "$60 a session." Seriously, that amount of money gave me all the scared and excited sensations she was talking about.

"That's great," she said, "but how much change are people going to receive for $60?"

Ah, I thought — this feels familiar. It was back to the

awareness that Gary had given me about my $25 movie ticket level of change. That's something to remember: Often it takes a while for us to really understand and undo something, especially when it comes to those ingrained habits and old patterns of thinking.

Here's what I did. I paused and got the energy of how much change people were receiving when I charged $25, and I knew the answer right away: very little.

Next, I got the energy of how much they'd receive if they paid me $60, and I realized they would receive a lot more, but also that I was capable of more. So I imagined what I could do for $80, and the jump in what people would receive from $60 to $80 was so big that I chose that. If you thought I was excited and scared by $60, imagine how $80 felt?!

Gary called and asked what figure I'd come up with, and I said, "Gary, this is so tough for me to ask for," honestly — I was shaking, and my molecules were vibrating. I took a breath and said, "$80."

"Okay," he said. However, fast-forward to the day of that advanced Access class. Gary started the class with an announcement, in which he introduced me to everyone and said how we'd only met recently but how in a short space of time I'd done some amazing things for him and his body. He told the class I was offering one-to-one sessions, and how usually I charged $120, "But," he added, "for you guys he'll do it for $80."

I'm sure the gulp in my throat was audible everywhere within a ten-mile radius. Hearing $120 associated with my name was like ... well, hard to put into words! Maybe you're getting the energy. If you think about it, this was almost five times as much as what I previously thought I was worth. There absolutely were no words.

The truth is I did 20 sessions during that first class and not one person paid me less than $120. In fact, some actually paid me *more* to reflect the change that they'd received. This was a pivotal moment in my life and my work as a healer, and such an acknowledgement of what I could do.

The change I created at $120 was greater than anything I'd had access to previously, and not only that, *my job was so much easier.*

Here's why: When somebody is willing to pay you enough, they've stepped through one of the barriers to entry for the change that they're asking for. In crossing that barrier and paying you enough, they're willing to receive more.

Letting your existing clients know your rates have increased

Increasing your rates can take a little, or a lot, of courage. Here's how I dealt with it. Even though I was exploring these new modalities and ways of initiating change with people's bodies, I still had my chiropractic practice. I knew I had to offer to work with my current patients from this new space of healing. The issue was they were paying me my old rate of $25, and here I was asking for $120. However — I'd seen what was possible and I couldn't go back.

I told my existing patients I'd been exposed to a new energy that had immense healing capacities and was so much fun to work with. I stated that my new rate was $120 a session, that it'd be one-to-one, and would last an hour. I told them that if they wanted to go on this journey, great, but if not, I'd be happy to refer them to another chiropractor in town.

90% of my clients stayed with me.

What was miraculous, and what was so wonderful for me, were the people who stayed with me got the change I always wanted to be able to give them in all my years as a chiropractor, but which $25 just didn't allow.

I was creating change in an hour which previously would have taken six months. Midway through sessions my clients would look at me with this wonderful, peaceful sort of glazed look in their eyes, and they'd say, "Whoa — I didn't know this was possible," and I'd say, "Neither did I. Isn't it awesome?"

I moved from a place of offering tiny, limited change to creating massive change for me and my clients, and I truly understood the value of getting out of my comfort zone financially.

Is it time for you to get out of your comfort zone?

Finding the sweet spot

Here are those two questions that you can use to set your rates:

1. What would be so exciting for me to charge that I feel almost scared to ask for it, but if I got it would make me so happy?

2. How much change can I deliver for that amount?

The aim is to find the sweet spot: Explore what's exciting to ask for, and then consider the amount of change that you can create for that sum of money.

Now, please have some awareness as you navigate this new

way of setting your rates! Sure, $1000 is incredibly exciting to ask for, but can you comfortably deliver $1000 of change?

On the other hand, you might find it very easy to deliver $50 of change, but does that amount excite you? If you charge $50, will you end up feeling resentful and bored? Are you capable of creating something closer to $100, or even $200, of change?

Only you know, and I recommend you play and have fun with this. If it's not coming easily to you, re-read this chapter and run the clearings as many times as you need.

To close this chapter, I'd like to share a story with you that really helped me accept that the money I earned as a healer had the capacity to make the life greater of someone very dear to me.

Changing my nephew's reality

My nephew is such a sweet, sweet kid. One of those brilliant kids. One of those kids who's like a savant. He is just so smart. And, like a lot of smart people, he's very curious and he just loves asking questions.

In kindergarten and first grade he had teachers who embraced him as the gift he is and who loved that he asked so many questions, but when he moved to second grade everything changed for him. The change stemmed from the fact that his new teacher took his frequent hand-raising and curious nature as a slight against her. In fact, she was so affronted by the fact he asked her questions that she believed he was trying to challenge and undermine her.

In this particular school at that time if a student did something to annoy the teacher, they'd be given a yellow card as a 'first warning,' and if they did something 'bad' again, they'd get a red card which meant they couldn't go to recess and they couldn't go to lunch.

Now, my nephew was getting red cards four days out of five. Within three weeks of starting second grade, he was coming home with his shoulders slumped, looking like an old man who'd been beaten down and hated his job and hated his life. And he was seven years old.

I saw this for what it was very quickly: unacceptable. I knew my nephew and I understood his true nature. I spoke to my sister about the possibility of getting him into a different school, knowing that if we could find a private school he'd be nurtured and allowed to see he's not a problem, that his questions were wonderful, and that he was a great kid, period.

At the time my sister didn't have the financial means to make such a big change … but I did. We discovered an incredible private school two miles from where they lived and made an appointment for him to visit. After just one day there he came back beaming. His shoulders were back. He was alive. He was the happy kid that he used to be. I knew what I had to do. "Sign him up," I told my sister, "he starts tomorrow." She said, "I can't afford this, Dain. I'd love to but I can't."

I'd already made up my mind. "This is between me and him, and I'm paying for it. He wants to go. You're my little sister, I love you, and this needs to be done because this will create a different future for this kid."

He's been flying high ever since. He's looking at getting a volleyball scholarship and he wants to be a healer, and here's the thing that fills me with joy: I look at what his future would have been like had I not been able to contribute, and I know it would have been a totally different place.

Charging for what you do is actually a gift to you and others

Isn't that an interesting perspective?

It's a gift to your clients because it allows them to open the door to receive massive change, far more than they will receive if you work on them for free or charge a pittance for what you do.

It's a gift for you because you get to have financial ease and peace of mind. And then, how much more at ease will you be when you're with your clients?

And then beyond that, **it's a gift for those you care about**. How much can you contribute to other people if you have ease financially? Maybe you have a nephew or a niece whose reality and future could change as a result of you having the financial resources to contribute to it.

When we take money off the table as this bad, terrible, vicious, mean and awful thing, we get to create so much more. For our clients, for us, and for those dear to us.

How does it get any better than that?

Creating The Future: From Theory To Practice

As we draw toward the closing pages of this book, I'd like to invite you to take a moment to get a sense of the world you'd like to create.

If you could create the world just as you'd like it to be, what would it look like? Feel like? Be like? Some of you might need a moment to tap into it; others will know right away. Close your eyes if you want.

Get the energy of that world. Notice it probably has a dynamic sense of peace to it, and a lot of ease. It's probably a place where we can get together and contribute to each other.

Maybe it has financial ease and abundance for you and everyone willing to receive it. Maybe it has a sense of communion and connection and lightness where healing is easy because fixed points of view are dissolving.

Once you have a sense of it, ask yourself, *What gift am I and what unique gifts do I offer to people that I have never acknowledged that will allow this world to actualize?*

Get a sense of that. Is that easy for you to do?

A lot of us have a tendency to believe that the greatest things about us are weaknesses. I work with so many kind and caring people, the type of people you only have to be around for a minute and all the wrongness, judgment and separation melts out of your world. And yet — they've invalidated this natural gift they have their whole life.

Have you done this too? Perhaps you've downplayed or made excuses for your kindness, or your humor, or your passion? What if instead of invalidating it you started embracing it?

Taking that sense of the world you'd like to create, and coupling that with your unique gifts, here's a question for you:

What three requests and demands can you make of you right now that will change the course of your future to be what you would actually like it to be?

We can talk and theorize about creating a greater future, but how often do we put our ideas into practice? How often do we make a demand of ourselves that we will do and be whatever it takes to create that greater future?

Would you like to address that now? If so, you could say this:

I will be and I will do and I will change whatever it takes to create the future that I know is possible. And I will be kind to myself along the way. And everything that doesn't allow that ... You know the rest.

Please note that final demand: to be kind to yourself. When you add that into the mix of everything we've learned on our journey so far, and you take it into the awareness you're accessing now of the world you'd like to create — you, my friend, become unstoppable.

My sincere hope is that you're really getting a sense of you as you actually are, and the contribution you came here to be.

Choose joy

Can you choose to have joy as you carve your way through life? Can a body whisperer be joyous, or is that inappropriate? Some of us have this idea that as healers, we're supposed to suffer, and we'd better keep on suffering until all suffering in the world is eliminated. *Then* we can choose joy for us. Makes sense, right? Um, no it does not!

> *Wherever you decided your job was suffering and that you're doing a really good job if you're suffering — know that you're not being the contribution you could be when you're suffering. Everything that is, times a godzillion, will you destroy and uncreate it please?* **Right and wrong, good and bad, POD & POC, all 9, shorts, boys and beyonds.**

I have the point of view that our job is actually to be joyful until everybody is willing to choose joy as well. We can be the inspiration for the joy and the peace and the ease that's possible for everyone, by being it ourselves. Showcasing it, if you like.

That's my sense of one of the greatest gifts you can be on this planet: You can show others what's possible. Show them you can have ease with your body, with gifting, with receiving. That you can have joy, space, ease and fulfillment. That you never have to go to the wrongness of you.

What if you being that inspiration is one of the fundamental ways of creating a better world?

Stepping into the Kingdom Of We

Have you heard about the Kingdom Of We? It's a place where everyone is included and no one and nothing is judged. Sounds a lot like consciousness, right?

Absolutely, because in essence, the Kingdom Of We functions from the consciousness that creates the awareness that we're all interconnected. We have a sense of communion and connection with everyone and everything, including the Earth beneath our feet, and everyone and everything we encounter.

How did we get so lucky?

At the other end of the spectrum, we have The Kingdom Of Me: a place which, as you might expect from its name, is all about the individual. It's a place run on judgment and point of view, and as such, conflict, separation and pain are rife there.

Which kingdom would you now like to choose to live in?

I believe it's finally time for the Kingdom Of We to show up. The space of the oneness where all of us can be the gift that we are to each other.

Join me there?

Can I just say …
Thank you!

Thank you to YOU for embarking upon this
very different journey. Thank you for being who
and what you are in the world right now.

—

Know that a kinder, gentler world of possibilities
is within our grasp.

—

What if you truly being you is the gift, the
change, and the possibility this world requires?
I am beyond honored to be on this journey with
you. I look forward to what we together will
create as the future. Because …

—

You know you're my people, right?

—

You're the ones creating a greater possibility for others and using your very being and energy to do it. You're the ones out there changing the world energetically by being something different, by inviting a different possibility into existence. You are that brilliant, that leading edge, that much of a gift.

—

Please choose joy. Be moved, be stirred, be inspired. Be curious, be open, be surprised.

—

*Hands up if you're
a body whisperer!*

Resources

Close-Up On The Clearing Statement

For those who'd like to know more about the individual words and phrases that make up the Access Consciousness Clearing Statement, you can read more on the following pages, or head to the Access website where you'll find a video of me explaining it a little more: *theclearingstatement.com*.

Here's the clearing statement:

Right and wrong, good and bad, POD & POC, all 9, shorts, boys and beyonds.

Let's look at those individual powerhouse words and phrases now.

Let's start with the Right and Wrong, Good and Bad

Right and Wrong, Good and Bad stand for your judgments about whatever you're letting go of.

The weird part is when we judge something to be bad, that's actually less limiting than when we judge something as good. When we judge something as bad, at least we're willing to change it. When we judge something as good, we won't let it change because finally we got something right!

So, the clearing statement undoes the judgments of something being Right or Wrong, Good or Bad and opens up the energetic space for change.

Now the POC and POD

The clearing statement takes you back to the Point of Creation (POC) — or the Point of Destruction (POD) — and undoes the limitations caused by the Point of Creation wherever it began.

Imagine you're walking on the road of your life, but in the middle of the road you have this big, old tree of limitation that you haven't been able to get around yet. On the right, there's a big, huge mountain you can't climb, and on the left, there's a drop-off cliff to nowhere.

What are you going to do?

Well, you could chop up the tree and try to make sure to get all the pieces and the stub and the roots … and yet, it usually regrows, as we know.

Instead, what if you could follow a leaf, down a branch, down the trunk, and go back in time to where the seed of limitation started and invite the seed to dissolve, go away, poof, by going back to the point of creation, wherever it was created.

What would happen to that tree of limitations? Gone instantly. That's what the clearing statement does. It's like pulling the bottom card out of a house of cards. The whole thing falls down!

The All 9

The "All 9" stands for 9 layers of this clearing statement. I played a big part in developing these 9 layers, and I don't even remember what they all are. So you don't have to either. Basically though, it's like this: We are looking to get the biggest scoop of crap and limitations out of the way every time we do this clearing statement, and to do this, we run through every layer that we know exists.

If we clear enough poo out of the way of your life, we'll find the pony called "You" in there somewhere!

And the Shorts

The "Shorts" stands for what's meaningful about it, and what's meaningless about it, along with the punishments and rewards for it.

We all get that it can stick with us if we make something meaningful, right? However, it is even worse when you make something meaningless that ISN'T. Any time you make something meaningless that isn't, it can come back and rain on your head like space debris.

A quick example: My best friend Gary, the founder of Access Consciousness, is an "Endian." He always rolls his toothpaste up from the end of the tube. Both of his wives were "squeeze it in the middle" types of people. When he would walk into the bathroom and they were squeezing the toothpaste in the middle, he would get upset or frustrated. But he thought to himself: "I can't be upset about this. This is meaningless."

For about six months, he threw his upset out into the universe like space debris, because it should be "meaningless." Until finally one day, after really being upset about something else, he yelled, "Darn it! Can't you squeeze the toothpaste tube right?!"

That's what happens when you make something meaningless that isn't: It goes out into the universe like space debris and then rains down on your head when you least expect it.

> *So everything you've decided was meaningless that actually wasn't meaningless to you, that actually had a meaning, will you now destroy and uncreate it please?* ***Right and wrong, good and bad, POD & POC, all 9, shorts, boys and beyonds.***

Then the Boys

The "Boys" are something called nucleated spheres. How many times have you been told you need to peel the layers of the onion to get to the core of the issue and you've peeled, and you've peeled, and you've peeled, and all you got were tears?

You've attended workshops and classes and meditation sessions … you do all that stuff and you feel like, "YES I AM FREE," because you finally popped one layer of that onion. And then, within days, it feels like it grows back and you feel like you haven't gotten anywhere.

That's because it's not an onion. It's an energetic structure that's called a nucleated sphere; the thing that you're trying to get to, and another one outside of that, and another one outside of that, and another one outside of that ad infinitum.

> *So how many onions have you peeled in the various lifetimes you've had that you're still trying to peel and peel, and all you get are tears? Think about all the nucleated spheres creating the tears that you thought were onions. Will you now destroy and uncreate these, please?* ***Right and wrong, good and bad, POD & POC, all 9, shorts, boys and beyonds.***

And the last part: the Beyonds

What is a "Beyond"? Well, have you ever had something that came up and it was like, "Aaargh!?" That was a Beyond: something that stops you in your tracks and takes you out of the present moment. It can be the moment you got fired, or when you learned of a loved one's death, the time you walked in on a partner with someone else, or when you realized you owed the bank more than you could ever earn. Beyonds are those things we experience which are beyond thought, beyond feeling and beyond emotion.

> _All the Beyonds — will you destroy them and uncreate them, please?_ **Right and wrong, good and bad, POD & POC, all 9, shorts, boys and beyonds.**

How's your head? It's totally fine if these words send you into a spin, I get it. But if you are willing to let them into your life, you can start creating the life you would like to choose — and that is when you, my friend, will soar.

How about you try it — just try and see what it can do.

You have nothing to lose but your limitations. How freeing, exciting and incredible is that? How inconceivable, unstoppable and liberated would you be then?

Is it your time to soar?

About the Author

Dr. Dain Heer is an international author, change-maker and co-creator of Access Consciousness, one of the largest personal development modalities. For more than 20 years, he has been traveling around the world facilitating classes and workshops, sharing his joyful approach to life and provocative perspectives on consciousness and creation.

Originally trained as a chiropractor, he has developed a completely different approach to healing; empowering and inspiring people to tap into and recognize their abilities and knowing. Heer is also a pioneer in the understanding of subtle energy and its effects on change, health and well-being and has developed his own process known as the Energetic Synthesis of Being (ESB).

Growing up in the ghetto in Los Angeles, Heer was exposed to constant mental, physical, emotional, sexual and monetary abuse from a young age. However, he never chose to be a victim. Instead, he discovered the power of personal transformation, allowance, courage and resilience. He has learned to transform life's challenges into a gift of strength.

Above all, Heer realized that his inherent deep caring for others had never faded. Over time, Heer recognized that he had the ability to empower people to heal themselves, by choosing to approach healing in a new and powerful way.

He uses a unique set of tools and provides step-by-step energetic processes to get people out of the conclusions and judgments that are keeping them stuck in a cycle of no choice – leading them into moments of awe that have the power to change anything.

Find out more about Dr. Dain Heer on *drdainheer.com*.

Meet Access Consciousness Online

AccessConsciousness.com

DrDainHeer.com

GaryMDouglas.com

BeingYouChangingTheWorld.com

ReturnOfTheGentleman.com

TourOfConsciousness.com

YouTube.com/drdainheer

Facebook.com/drdainheer

Facebook.com/accessconsciousness

YouTube.com/accessconsciousness

Other Books By Dain Heer

Dr. Dain Heer is the author and co-author of many books, many of them translated into several languages.

Being You, Changing the World
The Return of the Gentleman
Embodiment
The Baby Unicorn Manifesto
The Baby Dragon Manifesto
The Baby Stardust Manifesto
Magic. You Are It. Be It.
Right Riches for You
Talk to the Animals
Sex is Not a Four-letter Word, but Relationship Oftentimes Is
Living Beyond Distraction
The Ten Keys to Total Freedom
Money Isn't the Problem, You Are
The Home of Infinite Possibilities
Would You Teach a Fish to Climb a Tree?
A Drop in the Ocean
The Very Greatest Adventure … Is You Truly Being You

Through the Access Consciousness shop online you can find these and many other books that will allow you to dive deeper into different possibilities in areas like money, relationships, kids, addiction, bodies, grief, leadership and more.

Turn the page to a different possibility on
accessconsciousness.com/shop.